The Work of Ismar David

THE WORK OF

Ismar David

Selected by Helen Brandshaft

Edited by David Pankow

THE RIT CARY GRAPHIC ARTS PRESS

Rochester, New York · 2005

וְהָיָה כְּעֵץ שָׁתוּל
עַל־פַּלְגֵי מָיִם
אֲשֶׁר פִּרְיוֹ יִתֵּן בְּעִתּוֹ
וְעָלֵהוּ לֹא־יִבּוֹל
וְכֹל אֲשֶׁר־יַעֲשֶׂה יַצְלִיחַ:

תהילים א:ג

hE IS LIKE A TREE PLANTED
BESIDE STREAMS OF WATER,
THAT YIELDS ITS FRUIT IN SEASON,
WHOSE FOLIAGE NEVER FADES,
AND WHATEVER IT PRODUCES THRIVES.

Psalms 1:3

Table of Contents

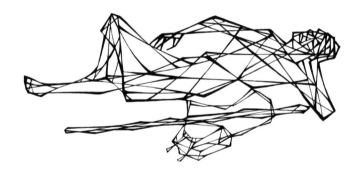

Foreword

MOST WELL KNOWN as a calligrapher, Ismar David was an artist and craftsman of extraordinary range and ability, who mastered a variety of media during the course of his long career. His accomplishments in book and type design, illustration, architecture, lettering and calligraphy are remarkable for their originality as well as for their high degree of execution. His sense of color and composition was exceptional, and no detail escaped his attention. A good deal of his work might be described as religious, and he received many commissions that called for designs with Biblical or sacred motifs. But to say that such work is religious alone is to diminish its character and meaning, for its appeal goes far beyond Judeo/Christian traditions and speaks to all who seek spiritual meaning in life.

My first extended exposure to the work of Ismar David came in 1980 when the Cary Graphic Arts Collection at Rochester Institute of Technology acquired a copy of *Our Calligraphic Heritage*, a carefully organized and detailed guide to the origins of the Roman alphabet and its subsequent development. The Cary Collection is situated in a university known for its printing and graphic design programs and already owned many books on the histories of writing, calligraphy, type design, and printing. An enthusiastic community of students looks to the collection's resources for inspiration and learning, as well as for an understanding of the history of their discipline. *Our Calligraphic Heritage*, therefore, proved to be a particularly apt acquisition and its virtues as a tool for teaching the history of the alphabet have been demonstrated many times over. To this day, it continues to be one of the three or four works I turn to when introducing students to the early development of letterforms.

In three parts, the work consists of an introductory text volume, a set of photographic reproductions of important developmental iterations of the Roman alphabet, and a portfolio of carefully rendered broadside models, each written by Ismar David in one of the scripts discussed in the text and frequently illustrated with his drawings. Text, reproductions, and broadsides are all gathered into an ingenious box, specially configured to display the contents. *Our Calligraphic Heritage* is clearly the work of someone intimately familiar with the challenges of teaching and the importance of exemplars. Most significantly, it contributes to a better understanding of the alphabet for the intrinsic beauty of its forms, its adaptation to different media, and its central role in communication. Many calligraphers have become teachers, and some have gone on to write instructional manuals, but only a handful, David among them, have produced works that so effectively serve their intended purpose. Indeed,

9

this sensitivity to purpose was characteristic of all of Ismar David's work, which included typography, designs for dust jackets, and myriad other applications.

In 1997, the opportunity to acquire Ismar David's archive for the Cary Collection was made possible through the generosity of his estate, in keeping with his own wish that his work be made available for study and research. A complementary archive, consisting primarily of his work in Hebrew letterforms and design, was donated to Yeshiva University in New York City, while a third archive of architectural drawings went to Columbia University.

Despite a thorough examination of the inventory description and even the many glimpses I had of David's work while helping to pack it for transport to Rochester, nothing could have prepared me for the thrill of examining at first hand, and at leisure, the rich contents of the archive—its trove of letterforms, both large and small, singly and in text; the drawings for Blaise Pascal's *Les Pensées*, published by the Limited Editions Club in 1971; the layouts for his great *Psalms* project, issued in 1973 by the Union of American Hebrew Congregations; the beautifully rendered artwork for his many dust jacket designs, and the designs for David Hebrew, a watershed type design issued by Intertype in 1954. Still a standard for Hebrew composition, this face is without a doubt Ismar David's most important and long-lasting contribution to the graphic arts, a design that David tried to make "free from corruptions that have beset Hebrew type development during the last centuries." The archive contains much important documentation for David Hebrew, including its development, proof stages, final release for machine composition, and more.

The Cary Collection is committed to sharing and promoting Ismar David's graphic legacy in a variety of ways. Fully cataloged, the archive is now completely accessible to users interested in exploring the work of this great designer. One of the most important aspects of the archive is its scope and comprehensiveness. Documenting David's entire career, it enables the student and scholar to understand his development as a designer and to appreciate his wide knowledge of media and techniques.

Plans to publicize Ismar David's graphic arts legacy are now underway, including exhibitions, a web-based, illustrated finding aid for the archive, and, of course, this publication, *The Work of Ismar David*. Organized into sections that document David's primary design interests, this volume is a visual record of his graphic achievement in all of its manifestations and also contains a biographical introduction and a bibliography of his published work. We are grateful to Jerry Kelly for providing a versatile design that gives full play to each image and to the Studley Press for its careful printing of the book and its many accompanying color illustrations.

Though historians of calligraphy and graphic design will certainly profit by an examination of *The Work of Ismar David*, we have deliberately made it available at a modest price, hoping that it will be used primarily as a practical text by students—for inspiration, for solutions to particular design problems, or just for the sheer enjoyment of looking at a life-work devoted to language in all of its literal and visual manifestations. It is a book that we are proud and honored to publish.

DAVID PANKOW, *Curator*
Cary Graphic Arts Collection

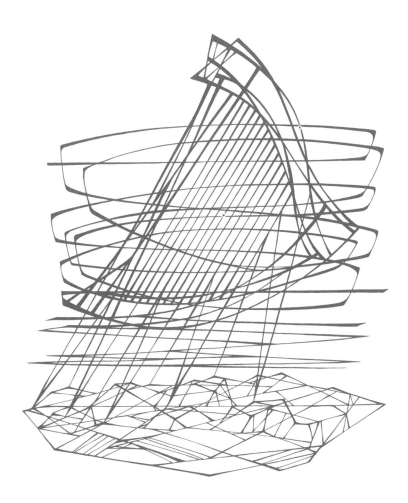

ISMAR DAVID
Berlin, ca. 1930

Questions are never indiscreet.
Only answers are.

I N 1932, aged 22 and about to finish art school in Berlin, Ismar David won an international competition to design the cover of a commemorative book for the Keren Kayemet Le-Israel, the Jewish National Fund. When the KKL asked him for advice in executing his proposal, Ismar offered to travel to Palestine to supervise production. No one could have foreseen the terrible events of the next thirteen years in Germany, but Ismar knew, as he put it, that he had no future in his homeland. He seized the chance to get out. He knew, too, that he would not see a single familiar face when he arrived in Jerusalem, but, as he would do twenty years later when he moved to New York, he left to better himself, to have more opportunities to do the work he knew he was capable of.

Drive, discipline and a distaste for what he called wishful thinking characterized the way Ismar lived and the way he worked. He was ferociously independent, relying on himself and his abilities, never accepting the conventional way of thinking as a matter of course, and above all, striving to express himself in his own unique graphic language.

No doubt work came first in Ismar's life. He kept a regular six-day-a-week studio schedule, beginning his workday at 9 in the morning with the first of two daily cigars (to help him concentrate, he claimed) and finishing up around 7 in the evening, but the long hours did not keep him from teaching or enjoying the company of others. A warm and vibrant man, with an ironic and often quirky sense of humor, he embraced life and savored its pleasures, like he savored the scotch that he drank every evening to palpable salutary effect. *"Trinkst, stirbst. Trinkst nicht, stirbst auch. So trinkst."* (If you drink, you die. If you don't drink, you die anyway. So you might as well drink.)

Although soft spoken and diminutive—Ismar would have said "average," but that would have been true only if you had been born on the short side of town—he was a force of nature. But a tidal wave or a hurricane has to start somewhere. Where did this mighty, occasionally stormy, highly motivated person come from? What helped make him the kind of man and artist he was?

Invariably, whenever someone approached him with, "Can I ask you a question?" he would smile and begin, "Questions are never indiscreet. Only answers are."

The official record of the Birth Registry of the City of Breslau states:

> Before the undersigned Registrar, there appeared today, duly identified, the business man Benzion Wolff David, residing in Breslau, Freiburgerstrasse 13, of Jewish religion, who reported that:
>
> His wife, Rosa David, née Freund, of Jewish religion, residing with him, had given birth in Breslau in his residence, on August 27, 1910, at 8:30 A.M. to a child of male sex and that the child had been given the name of Joseph Ismar.

Wolff David sold insurance, a modest enterprise sustained for the most part through the good will of a circle of friends who insured shipments of goods for their own businesses. He had come from northern Germany to Breslau, the "Berlin of the East," a jewel of culture, learning and commerce that attracted many Europeans for whom the German national capital was out of reach. There, he met Rosa Freund, a school teacher whose large and prominent family lived in the surrounding area, and the couple married when Wolff was 37 and Rosa a few days shy of 32. She was 35 when she gave birth to their second son, Hebrew name Joseph Israel but called Ismar after his mother's brother, in the *hinterhaus* (back house) of a middle-class apartment building near the center of town.

Ismar's early childhood memories naturally centered around life at home; playing with his older brother Felix and their younger sister Selma, to whom he was especially close, and traditional Jewish domestic practices. He watched his mother use a feather to brush egg wash over the challah dough, and he trembled with the rest of the household at the calamity if the dough failed to rise. The family lived according to Jewish law and celebrated the Jewish holidays with devotion, storing the pieces of their own *sukkah* in the basement of the apartment building. For *Sukkot*, the Feast of the Tabernacles, the family assembled the little booth on their balcony where they decorated it, taking their meals there during the week-long holiday.

As a member of the *Hevra Kaddisha* (sacred society), a group of volunteers who share the duties of cleansing and preparing the dead for burial, Wolff performed some of the community's most holy rites. He was strictly observant and would have found it as shocking to learn that any of his children had entered a Reformed synagogue as to discover that they had gone into a church. Yet, as an emancipated German Jew, he maintained a stylish mustache and goatee (an imperial), using a foul-smelling depilatory on his face to avoid violating religious laws against shaving. And he would not have considered wearing a yarmulke in the street or exposing the fringes of his prayer shawl to public view.

In an era of unprecedented intellectual and social advancement in Germany, Rosa and Wolff David took justifiable pride in their nation and its achievements, embracing what was great and good, and sometimes merely conventional there. They participated in the cultural activities of their city. The classics of German literature lined their bookshelves. Bohemian glass adorned their home. However, Rosa and Wolff forbade Ismar, Felix and Selma such "vulgar" fare as Karl May's popular novels of the American West. And, although Rosa and Wolff would never have allowed their children to read *Struwwelpeter,* little Selma ate from dishes decorated with a sanitized verse about the characters from Heinrich Hoffmann's gruesome children's book:

Die Suppe ist ein gut' Gericht,	Soup is a good dish,
Nur Suppen-Kaspar mag sie nicht.	But Soupy-Kaspar doesn't like it.
Gemüs' und Fleisch bekommt nur der,	Vegetables and meat are only served,
Der seine Suppe aß vorher.	After his soup is finished.
Wenn dein Teller ist geleert,	When your plate is clean,
Wird dir noch Kompott beschert.	You'll be given dessert.

Ismar had not quite reached his fourth birthday when World War I engulfed Europe. Wolff, in his forties and not immediately subject to conscription, contributed to the war effort in the ways that an ordinary citizen could. Ismar remembered, not without irony, his father's patriotic watch chain with the fob that read, *"Gold gab ich für Eisen"*—I gave gold for iron. Eventually, as the fighting took its devastating toll, Germany dug deeply into its human reservoir. Wolff was drafted, but in deference to his age and experience, or perhaps merely because he could read and do sums, he was made a kind of quartermaster. Wolff later told the family about his fellow draftees, recruits so raw that they literally did not know their right hands from their left; to help them execute maneuvers, they were given straw to hold in one hand and told to turn straw. Sent to Romania, Wolff remained stationed there until the end of the war.

While her husband served the Fatherland, Rosa David took care of the household and the insurance business. A *kinderfräulein* took care of the three children. Felix, Ismar and Selma adored the young woman who looked after them. They especially enjoyed excursions to her parents' home at a railway station outside the city. It seemed to Ismar that station masters must always have little vegetable gardens allotted to them, as he could see the cultivated plots near the tracks at each stop. The consequence, in this instance, was that the delighted children could eat homegrown treats.

The modest variety of country food provided a stark contrast with the bill of fare in town: principally large, woody turnips prepared in every way domestic ingenuity could devise. German propaganda extolled the virtues of *eintopfgerichte,* one-pot meals, the main ingredient of which seemed to be resourcefulness. German housewives also made do with poor quality bread, baked with unrefined flour in order to

Ismar, Selma, and Felix with their *kinderfräulein* ca. 1914.

extend the flour and sold, by government mandate, three-days-old in order to allow the thinnest possible slices. Ismar picked the chaff from his teeth as he ate his meager portion. Fortunately, from Romania, Wolff was able to supplement the family diet with packets of dried beans which Rosa sometimes used to make a cake.

After the collapse of the German army and the signing of the Armistice of 1918, a newly discharged Wolff, ill with recurrent fevers, walked home to Breslau. Distressed about the unjewishness of his life during the war, he was reluctant to resume his activities with the *Hevra Kaddisha*, but his colleagues eventually prevailed upon him to continue. Physically, though, Wolff was a changed man. He never fully recovered his health, and year by year, the family witnessed his slow deterioration.

Still, the end of the war brought relief and plenty of new experiences. A Jewish organization sent children, Ismar among them, on vacations to host families outside of Germany. The "starving war child" remembered the unfailing kindness and generosity of his hosts. During one of these trips, Ismar saw his first opera, *Boris Godunov*, and on another trip, to Vienna, he and a companion ran off for a day to see Schönbrunn Palace. Rosa and Wolff, too, were eager to provide Felix, Ismar and Selma with some of the things that they had not been able to enjoy during the war. But these delicacies held little appeal for the children who had no idea they had been missing anything. Wolff and Rosa took the children to a bakeshop, only to be disappointed when Selma, trying whipped cream for the first time, gravely pronounced that it tasted like soap.

As Rosa directed more and more of her attention to her husband's declining health, the children pitched in with office chores where they could. In 1923, the year Ismar turned 13, the children's assistance became absolutely essential because they were the only ones in the family able to cope with the wildly proliferating zeros of Germany's hyperinflation. The old joke about the man who leaves a wheelbarrow full of money unattended, and returns to find the money dumped on the ground and the wheelbarrow stolen, rings too true. A cash gift for Ismar's bar mitzvah metamor-

16

phosed from a suitcase to, in his words, "a little wallet" because Wolff waited until the next day to make the purchase. In a few short months, Germany was forced to drastically accelerate the production of paper currency by printing it only on one side. Using the blank side of the bill as drawing paper, Ismar infuriated his father who could not grasp that the bank notes were worth less than the paper they were printed on. The crisis ended in December with the introduction of the *rentenmark* which replaced the old *reichsmark* at a rate of 1:1,000,000,000,000,000.

In 1919 Ismar had followed his brother into König Wilhelm Gymnasium Presumably hoping to mitigate some of the adversities facing a Jewish child in public school, Ismar's parents sent him there because Felix had had a good experience with a sympathetic teacher the year before. But whereas Felix triumphed academically with little effort, the curriculum utterly defeated his brother. Quick at mathematics and a good chess player, Ismar understood the structure of things but was a slow reader. Although in later life he would appreciate the beginnings of the classical education he had received (some familiarity with the underpinnings of Latin and the Greek alphabet helped him to study manuscripts), Ismar could not have been a more lamentable or unhappy student. One of his French compositions had so many mistakes that the teacher returned it with the comment "*Unkorrigierbar*" (uncorrectable) written across on the top.

Seventy years later, Ismar still mimicked that ancient French teacher who bored students with his experiences "*in der sonn-nn-igen Proven-nn-ce*" (in sunn-nn-y Proven-nn-ce). Ismar had the bad luck to attend school at a time when an entire generation of teachers had been eradicated by war, only to be replaced by the superannuated or the inept. In addition, surgery at age ten for a crossed left eye corrected Ismar's appearance, but despite patches and other training methods, he never learned to see with both eyes simultaneously. (Interestingly, he thought that the resultant lack of depth perception may have contributed to his affinity for line.) Perhaps the trials he endured after the surgery helped doom his academic career. For some time, double vision plagued him. Whatever the underlying cause, Ismar's formal education ended at age fourteen, and his happiest school day was his last.

In 1925, Ismar entered an apprenticeship to a house painter. The master and other apprentices were Gentiles and the workweek included Saturdays. Rosa and Wolff understood at the outset that their son would no longer be able to fully observe Jewish law, yet they made the arrangements for his training. Perhaps Wolff accepted the necessity of the situation because he had long before come to grips with his own compromises during the war. Plainly, Ismar had no chance to succeed as a scholar.

In those days before latex paint, house painting required specialized technical knowledge and meant hard physical labor for the apprentices. However, Ismar learned about paint vehicles, varnishes and finishes—experience and information that would serve him throughout his career. He also learned things he hoped never to use again, the day the master dispatched him to help a *kammerjäger* (chamber hunter). The German word for exterminator is charming; the real-life battle with bed bugs, anything but. For Ismar, the important thing was that a journeyman's papers would supply the necessary credentials for further studies in art school.

After completing his apprenticeship in 1928, Ismar left for Berlin, where the social and professional aspects of his life changed decidedly for the better. He joined the affectionate family circle of his uncle, Ismar Freund, a leader in Berlin's Jewish community and an influential writer of laws pertaining to Jews throughout Europe. Ismar became more publicly active, taking part in some of the election activities of his uncle, skiing and hiking with his cousins, and even painting scenery for a Jewish cabaret. In a letter to his aunt and cousins at the time of his uncle's death in 1956, Ismar wrote:

> You gave me the warmth of family life and education. I can still see in my mind's eye the afternoons of the Sabbath and I hear Uncle Ismar reading the Bible. The evenings of music with the different (at that time young) musicians and their audience appear out of the past. . . . In every facet of those times I see Uncle Ismar as the family father and the organizer in the Jewish community. I was never able to express my gratitude for all I received from you then, and which has been a foundation for my later life…

Unable to enter art school on his arrival in Berlin, Ismar did not waste time. Typically, he took a critical look at himself. Concluding that the commonest newspaper illustrator had more skill as a draftsman than he did, he took several months of intensive private instruction in drawing to better prepare himself for more formal study.

Later in 1928, Ismar entered the Städtische Kunstgewerbe- und Handwerkerschule Berlin, Charlottenburg, Berlin's municipal school for arts and crafts, where he received excellent training and met like-minded individuals. Intensely motivated, the students pursued color work by day and shifted to black-and-white work by night. Early on, Ismar had thought to become a portrait artist, but at the school in Charlottenburg he studied decorative painting, an applied art, which did more to develop his natural inclinations and in the end opened wider fields for him.

Two of his professors especially impressed Ismar. He never forgot Hans Orlowski's dedication to teaching and his sensitivity to the problems of students. (An edition of the Psalms with woodcuts by Orlowski was in Ismar's library.) But it was Johannes Böhland who awakened his student to the importance of understanding culture and tradition in the letterforms used in writing. Ismar learned to see their harmony and rhythm, richness of form, and possibilities of expression. These seeds grew into

Ismar's own philosophy of writing, as he expressed in a letter to Böhland in the 1950s:

> I'd like to try to formulate my point of view (as far as it concerns the area of writing) which came to me gradually, and surely coincides with yours, as follows: we should study and absorb the development of writing styles, and try to understand the cultural epochs that these styles reflect. But then we should try to express them in a new way that mirrors our own feeling and time and reverberates with the pulse of our own era. Even if we do not reach the perfection of form of the best classical models, we must keep writing alive and fill the way we use forms with new life. Writing should not only be a technical necessity for the purpose of communication, but rather, a vivid form of art that is recreated in each generation.

Ismar completed his course of study and, in 1932, left for Palestine to advise the Keren Kayemet on producing his design for the Golden Book. After the kind of sea voyage where the passengers emerge grateful to be merely filthy and sick, he presented himself at the headquarters for the Keren Kayemet in Jerusalem. Two sisters working there assured him that adjustment to life in Palestine would be easy—after all he had studied for his bar mitzvah and he already knew Hebrew. As plausible as this sounded in the office, the reality outside, where the spoken language was quite

Pencil drawing, ca. 1930.

In Palestine, ca. 1935.

different from the Ashkenazic Hebrew he had learned at home, was another matter. But Ismar quickly joined Jerusalem's sizable German émigré community, in which language posed no barrier. His earliest friend there, Charlotte Stern, already a Jerusalemite of several years standing, owned Charlotte's Gifts on Storrs Street.

Under British administration since 1922, Palestine had been designated to become the Jewish national home, with provisions protecting the rights of all inhabitants, regardless of race or religion. It was a magical place for Ismar, a place of new experiences and delicious freedom. He found work. He found women. And women found him. After his first love abandoned him when her previous boyfriend arrived in the country, Ismar found he was apparently quite irresistible. The young newcomer enjoyed a lively year before settling down in a long-lasting relationship with another German expatriate. In 1936, Itamar (the Hebrew form of Ismar) David opened his studio in the basement of their apartment building in the Rosh Rehavia section of Jerusalem. Austere Palestine had little use for the decorative painting in which he had trained, so Ismar turned to graphic and interior design.

The exposure to the culture, atmosphere and appearance of Palestine profoundly affected Ismar and gave him a fresh perspective. The rugged terrain, translated into linear terms, reverberates in many of the religious illustrations he would do throughout the remainder of his life. Ismar found himself, too, in the midst of a cultural revival. As early as 1933, he began to envision a new Hebrew typeface, one inspired not by European models but by earlier writing of the Middle East.

> Working in the graphic field made me wish for Hebrew types that would be in harmony with the modern spirit that was to transform Hebrew into an every-day language. But what printers had to offer then were poor traditional faces or even poorer modernistic ones. The task I then set for myself was designing a type family consisting of a book face based in its shadings on the written form, a slanted version to function the way italic does and an even stroke version, the equivalent of a sans-serif. Each of these variations was planned in three weights—light, medium and bold. For

many years, on and off, I worked on these designs and their refinement. I pasted up endless advertisements to test their acceptability, as they departed decisively from types then commonly in use.

He wanted "to enable every printer in the country to produce well planned and well organized printing for books and commerce, aesthetically comparable to printing with Roman type." Early generations of the letterforms that would become the typeface David Hebrew appear in Ismar's commercial work, beginning in the mid-1930s.

The Palestine Mandate recognized English, Hebrew and Arabic as the three official languages of the country, so Ismar accordingly studied English and tried to learn Arabic calligraphy. He abandoned the latter effort after concluding that he would not be able to absorb Arabic culture fully enough to do justice to its writing. He did design some trilingual and many bilingual advertisements, as well as stationery, signboards and a wide variety of graphics for private industry and government and cultural institutions. The Keren Kayemet commissioned several more Golden Book covers and Hebrew University used his services. Ismar's corporate clients included The Lud Cigarette Factory, Blue Band Margarine, Kaiser Fraser automobiles, Nesher Cement Works, Universitas Booksellers, and the printing and publishing concern of M. Pikovsky, Ltd. As might be expected in a small city like Jerusalem, he often became friendly with the people who ran those businesses.

At this time, residents of the Middle East could not go to a store to buy a table or a suit of clothes because ready-made goods were simply not available. (Ismar would say with a kind of sheepish pride that in Palestine he had his apparel tailor-made right down to the silk underwear.) Consequently, Ismar's work encompassed any type of design his clients needed. He designed furniture for the home of his friend Ferri Friedman, who with his father and brother owned S. Friedman, Ltd., a stove manufacturer. (Their three figures appear in Ismar's design for the company's trademark.) He designed the interior of the offices of the Greek Patriarch. (On a visit to Israel years later, Ismar saw that the ceiling light he designed was still there, although apparently not dusted in the interval.) He also designed the exterior lettering for the Weizmann Institute, and many installations for trade and cultural expositions.

During his twenty years in Jerusalem, Ismar took in as many of the sights as possible, experiencing the natural and sometimes unnatural local phenomena. He bicycled down to the Dead Sea—the only place where he could float, since he was never able to learn to swim—and, as was customary, took the bus with the bicycle strapped on top back up to Jerusalem. He stayed a night in the guest hut of a monastery, one of several in the country that are built into sheer walls of rock. Broken windows in the hut, in this era before the pesticide DDT, meant countless insects crunching under foot as he entered. The way Ismar told it, this extraordinary setting was a punishment facility for monks who had transgressed their vows or had gone insane, and the night echoed with the howls of the inmates in their surrounding cell-caves.

Travels included Palestine's neighboring countries, too. Passing through Syria, Ismar had the rare opportunity to see a private collection of ancient Roman glass. He spent a month working on a book project in Lebanon and recalled with warmth the friendly reception of the Lebanese people who went out of their way to offer the Palestinian Jew arak to drink in the cool misty shade created by giant waterwheels.

Ismar had always enjoyed speed, and among other adventures, briefly knew the thrill of driving his own car. Regrettably, the thrill was brief. The man who had sold Ismar his 1938 Ford hadn't actually owned it and the stolen vehicle had to be returned to the man who did.

Despite hardships and periodic disturbances in Palestine, the relative freedom Ismar experienced in the Middle East sharply contrasted with his family's circumstances in Europe. He later said that his father, who died in 1930, would never have understood subsequent events in Germany. The resurgence of anti-Semitism that followed World War I rapidly and dramatically escalated after 1933. As the political situation for Jews deteriorated, Ismar struggled to make arrangements for his mother, his brother Felix, and his sister Selma to emigrate to Palestine. In fact, Felix and his wife visited Jerusalem to explore the possibility of moving there, but Felix saw himself as a respected teacher in Germany and was unwilling to risk starting over elsewhere. His wife's parents, who already lived in Palestine, pleaded with Ismar to persuade their son-in-law to emigrate. But Felix had made up his mind; he and his wife returned to Germany. When conditions became intolerable there in 1938, they turned on the gas in their home, killing themselves and their small children.

Almost all of Ismar's mother's ten brothers and sisters and over 150 cousins perished under the Nazi regime. One cousin had enough sense to send his children to Canada, but believing that the storm would eventually blow over, not enough sense to leave himself. Rosa's brother Ismar Freund and his family emigrated to Palestine. Rosa herself, who had refused to leave Germany while she had children living there, barely managed to escape at the eleventh hour with Selma and Selma's husband and child. The four of them spent the war years stranded in Japanese-occupied Shanghai.

On the other side of the world, pre-war New York hosted the 1939 World's Fair. In March, Ismar arrived in the city to supervise the installation of his design for the exhibition inside the Palestine Pavilion. It was his first trip to the United States, but numerous delays, the irritating requirements of local unions, and the consequent furious work schedule left him little time to see much more of his surroundings than his hotel in Manhattan and the subway line to the fairgrounds in Queens. Ismar managed, however, to initiate discussions with Intertype Corporation about his typeface,

David Hebrew. Once the exhibition was installed, Ismar returned to Palestine, still under British mandate, a few months before the outbreak of the Second World War.

Following an initial period of economic uncertainty, the war years became almost a boom time for Palestine as an important military headquarters and staging area for materiel and personnel. Jerusalem was enlivened by the high-spirited Australians stationed there. Fond of harmless pranks, they lifted lightweight cars off the street and put them on the sidewalk for fun. Ismar befriended one Aussie soldier, a sign board painter in civilian life who did not consider himself especially gifted but wanted to learn as much as possible in order to help his talented daughter when he returned home. Touched, Ismar gave the man private instruction.

Occasionally during the war, rumors of an enemy advance caused some people to panic and liquidate their possessions for ready cash. So it happened that a Dürer folio found its way into the hands of a friendly bookseller who offered the volume to Ismar on an installment plan. But buying on credit was not the sort of thing a well brought-up German boy did. Although he rued the Dürer that got away, he eventually consoled himself with an Aldine incunabulum, purchased at an AIGA auction in the fifties. Not an avid collector per se, Ismar occasionally purchased things that interested him, like this edition of Saint Augustine's *Confessions* by Aldus Manutius, a craftsman of conviction, whose books combined utilitarian and aesthetic ideals that Ismar admired.

In 1947 Ismar made a second trip to New York. This time, he came to investigate printing methods in the United States and took the opportunity to resume the war-interrupted negotiations with Intertype Corporation about David Hebrew. He also came to meet his mother who was arriving in New York via train from California. The Jewish Agency had arranged for her passage from Shanghai to Palestine. Ismar's sister Selma and her family had decided to emigrate to Australia where Selma's husband had family, so Rosa traveled alone. As the crowd cleared from the platform at the train station, Ismar saw his mother for the first time in fifteen years. A small woman, she carried a large bag that she had dragged across three continents for him. When she gave her son the down from a comforter, the carefully preserved remnant of her European existence, he hardly knew whether to laugh or cry. Ismar and his mother left for Palestine, where she remained until her death in 1956.

After the November 1947 United Nations resolution that partitioned Palestine into Jewish and Arab states, hostilities erupted and Israel's War of Independence began. Fighting was intense and in the spring of 1948, the Arab Legion captured the Old City, laying siege to the remainder of Jerusalem. With supplies of food, fuel and water severed, conditions became so dire that it seemed quite rational to consider whether it was worth going through an area known to harbor snipers in order to find a tree rumored to have edible leaves. As one of Ismar's friends dryly commented, it was very interesting to witness the birth of a state, but not recommended.

Struggle did not cease with statehood. In its early years, Israel faced formidable political and economic difficulties that were mirrored in the lives of its citizens who had to cope with shortages of food, other supplies and housing, as well as heavy taxation and severe monetary restrictions. Massive immigration put retail space in Jerusalem in short supply, and Ismar found himself working almost around the clock planning the division and subdivision of stores. The authorities commissioned him to design graphics, currency and stamps for the new state which now needed the normal accessories of government and society.

In the early spring of 1951 Ismar welcomed the opportunity for a break and returned to New York to sign a contract with Intertype for David Hebrew. The final drawings for the book face and its accompanying italic (both in light weight only) were delivered between 1951 and 1952 with the help of Robert Leslie of The Composing Room, a progressive typographical concern on 46th Street. Intertype issued David Hebrew in 1954. Two years later, Ismar described the financial rewards of a type designer, "At the moment, the type exists only in the form of 12 pt. upright and italic Intertype matrices. . . . Intertype has the rights for line casting and photo-setting machines only. I have the right to royalties for 10 years. So far, after two years of the type's existence: $20."

Ismar's skills as an exhibition designer brought him back to New York in 1952 to work for the Bonds of Israel campaign. Again, his schedule was hectic, and the design and installation of an effective display took much longer than expected. "I think I had the busiest time of my life in these 9 months I have worked for the Israel Bond Drive," he wrote to a friend in Israel. "If I would try to write a book of all my experiences of this time, people would take it only as fiction."

The plans for the Israel Exposition for the State of Israel Bonds went awry almost immediately. When the original conception of a traveling exhibition mounted in two railway cars proved unfeasible, the organizers regrouped to consider a caravan of six large trailers. Finally, they settled for a stationary display. Finding an exhibition space available for only two months in New York was difficult; Ismar himself finally found the location (on 48th Street off Fifth Avenue) and construction began in a hurry. "I went through troubles," he wrote to a friend. "I worked day and night like in Israel." He also worked on some promotional material and show windows for the exhibition. The sponsors then arranged for a second presentation. "Both exhibitions have been a success," he informed a colleague in Israel. "The second one, which has its first showing in Miami, is much nicer than the first one. Partly because the exhibits you collected are nicer and partly because mistakes I made the first time I didn't repeat the second time. On the contrary, I was able to use the experience of the first and improve the design."

During this same period, Ismar grappled with preparing an exhibition of his own work for the Jewish Museum, as well as producing graphic work for the Bonds, for himself, and for a few other clients. He further reported to his friend in Israel, "By working on those projects I feel like [I did as] a schoolboy many years ago. I have to learn how to prepare work for representation and how to prepare work for reproduction." Frequently needing the typesetting and printing services of The Composing Room, Ismar spent time with its publicity director, Hortense Mendel.

The United States in 1952, especially New York City, was full of possibilities for Ismar. Israel, in those early years, had no need for the kind or quality of work that he wanted to do. In demand there, sometimes working "day and night," Ismar did not have jobs that presented the kind of challenges he sought. In addition, scarce materials and unskilled labor made it difficult to achieve even a minimum standard. Although Ismar felt a strong attachment to Israel as a haven for a people who were accepted nowhere else, "in the end," he wrote to a friend, "we have to live our own life as best as we can and where we think we can achieve our best." America offered him the chance to "achieve his best." Then too, his relationship with Hortense Mendel had intensified: they had decided to marry, and Ismar felt that Israel would be too Spartan for her.

The marriage was the first for both Ismar, 42, and Hortense, who was nine years his senior. At the ceremony on June 3, 1953, the rabbi had to ask the nervous bride twice to remove her gloves in order for Ismar to place the ring on her finger. The couple settled into Hortense's apartment on Jerome Avenue in the Bronx. The marriage lasted until 1960 when, after they had spent a beautiful day together in the country, Hortense died suddenly of a heart attack.

Like others who aspired to become Americans in 1953, Ismar needed to prove himself not only employable but also employed. Publisher Harry N. Abrams gave him his first official job in the United States, satisfying immigration requirements and enabling him to move here. Despite a bad reputation among artists, Harry was fair with Ismar and paid his invoices on time. Ismar opened his studio on West 46th Street and with Hortense's help sent letters of introduction to potential clients.

Because of his experience with Hebrew lettering, Ismar had initially expected to make his living working for synagogues—after all, he reasoned, there were more Jews in New York than all of Israel. He designed decorative elements for several synagogues in various parts of the country, at times working with the architects Percival Goodman and Sidney Eisenstadt. But after a few disagreeable experiences with some rabbis, Ismar concentrated on graphic work for publishers.

Book jacket lettering, at that time, was customarily done by hand. Almost immediately, Ismar's involvement with historical writing styles deepened, due in part to the beginning of his teaching career. Graphic artist George Salter, a fellow émigré who taught at Cooper Union, recommended Ismar as a calligraphy instructor there in 1953. Ismar used to say that he was forced to begin a more intensive study of letterforms in order to stay one step ahead of his students.

Cooper Union, like European arts and crafts schools, employed working artists as instructors. Ismar felt very much at home in this environment where his first priority was to provide his students with the skills and foundation that they would need in professional life. Introducing himself to his class, he explained the value of understanding letterforms:

> Now it is my job again to make you more conscious of these forms. We will notice nuances of measurements and proportions of letterforms, [and] by seeing and producing them, you will train your eye and your hand—but most important, your mind. You will develop your judgment and your taste, which you will need whenever you are confronted with problems of lettering. And like all knowledge, you will find that this will help you in other problems of aesthetics.

Each year Ismar asked to teach a night class, which he found particularly rewarding. His night students of 1965 stood out in his memory. They returned his affection, and at the end of the term, gave their instructor a book about the history of writing that he treasured the rest of his life.

Now established in America, Ismar vacationed in places across the country, in Europe and in Israel, first with Hortense and later with his second wife, Dorothy Hoffman, whom he married in 1962. Over the years, he made regular visits to Rockport, Massachusetts, where he relaxed and painted landscape watercolors for pleasure. On a 1966 trip to England, he had the breathtaking experience of seeing original Leonardo and Holbein drawings for the first time. Ismar admired artists with strong personalities, particularly Leonardo. In Milan, seeing the little more than fragmentary remains of *The Last Supper* moved him deeply. In Washington D.C.'s National Gallery, he liked to visit the portrait of Ginevra de' Benci, the only Leonardo painting in the United States, and appreciate the almost imperceptible subtleties of the glazes on her throat. Other old friends were the Rembrandts, the El Grecos and a little painting by Sasetta, all at the Metropolitan Museum in New York. In Florence, he loved to see the work of Botticelli and, to his delight and amazement one time in Rome, he stumbled upon Bramante's *Tempietto*, tucked away in the courtyard of San Pietro in Montorio.

In the late 1960s, Cooper Union changed from a professional crafts school into a college and dispensed with the services of its instructors, even dedicated teachers like

Teaching a workshop, ca. 1970.

Ismar. At about the same time and for no apparent reason—it may have been a generational shift among art directors—Ismar's book jacket work dried up. Greatly disheartened by both the loss of the interchange with students and the mainstay of his livelihood, Ismar made use of the extra time to produce a series of fifty-eight illustrations for *The Psalms*. He took on the work, first as a commission, but when that fell through, completed it on his own. Two years in the making, the drawings were displayed at various exhibition spaces in an effort to expose the work of the artist and find a publisher for the series.

Ismar had arrived at the stage of his career where he felt, "As my convictions about my own style deepened and crystallized I became rather selective in the kind of drawings I was prepared to do. [I was] waiting always for the opportunity to do, without compromising, what I thought could become my contribution in this field." The Limited Editions Club offered him a project of this caliber when it commissioned him to illustrate Blaise Pascal's *Les Penseés*, published in 1971. The resulting twelve compositions are among Ismar's proudest and finest achievements.

He responded wholeheartedly to Pascal's character and conviction. Never rigid or parochial in his views of religion, Ismar had a broad knowledge and open-mindedness that caused him to respect other beliefs. "I found reading Pascal and about Pascal very stimulating," he wrote to a friend. "If one overlooks the bickering of the seventeenth century one finds wonderful formulations of ideas and a great integrity well expressed by a deep believer in his faith." He further explained:

> To create illustrations for Pascal has been a real challenge to me. I felt immediately committed to convey the deep religiosity, the compassion and the purity of thought of this man that reaches out from the seventeenth century into our time. I have strived to find for these drawings the style in which timelessness is fused with contemporary form of expression. I felt that that is part of Pascal who was rooted in sources of Christianity but was concerned about the living generation and its future. A line pattern, simple but involved, clear but suggestive, should bring Pascal to life, whose thoughts also were clear and simple, but involved and sometimes even emotional. The colors should help to create a mood but remain abstract as pure thoughts are. . . . Reading Pascal, one is filled with the conviction that this man was true to himself uncompromisingly. While it did not seem essential to live an ascetic life, he was convinced that only a spiritual life is worth living. So to create compositions accompanying Pascal, I became convinced that one can only do justice to *Les Penseés* by symbolically presenting Pascal's personality and not physical things or locales.

The themes expressed in the illustrations for *Les Penseés* so fascinated Ismar that he dreamed of basing large-scale paintings on them, if and when he ever retired.

In 1973, the Union of American Hebrew Congregations decided to celebrate its hundredth anniversary by publishing an edition of *The Psalms* using Ismar's drawings and a new translation prepared by the Jewish Publication Society. Ismar designed the book and made additional decorative elements. Choosing David Hebrew and Monotype Dante for the typefaces, he laid out the bilingual text in a format he had pioneered with his contribution to *Liber Librorum*, a 1955 collection of sample Bible designs commemorating the four-hundredth anniversary of Gutenberg's Bible. Ismar considered *The Psalms* his most intensely personal work.

> Two elements are fused: the absorption of the Psalms as part of my Jewish heritage with my desire to communicate the impressions these made on me in my own language. This is, according to my own nature, graphic. The lines do not define forms but, like the lines of letterforms or other symbols, they have to become symbols themselves. At the same time, they have to form abstract patterns of harmony and be expressive according to the contents of the theme that underlies each composition.

The Psalms brought the artist's career full circle by combining his early work, David Hebrew, with his mature style and illustration ideas. The American Institute of Graphic Artists selected it as one of the fifty best books of the year.

The Psalms did nothing, however, to revive Ismar's book jacket career. Fortunately, architectural design for cemeteries had begun to make up for the loss of work in publishing. Back in 1953, Leon Shipper had commissioned Ismar to design a feature with

28

In front of the glass chapel at Beth Israel Cemetery, 1966.

a bronze bas-relief map of ancient Israel for the grounds of Beth Israel Memorial Park in Woodbridge, New Jersey. Eleanor Roosevelt (!) stood in front of the monument and spoke at its dedication. More projects followed. The free-standing glass chapel that Ismar designed for Beth Israel has fallen into disrepair, but his design work on the grounds and in the mausoleums there, including a quotation from the 23rd Psalm in large letters on dramatically striated black and white stone, can still be seen.

In 1965, Alfred Locke, owner of Pinelawn Memorial Park in Farmingdale, Long Island, approached Ismar about a centerpiece for an area on the grounds of the non-sectarian cemetery. Using John Donne's "No man is an island" text, the theme chosen by Mr. Locke, Ismar designed a mausoleum with the quotation inscribed on its 50' x 13' façade. His first assignment at Pinelawn reflects the way he thought about architectural design:

> When you work in stone, then you have to forget about the effects of the moment and feel instead that you are responsible for something more permanent. Something that in twenty years, people will still be able to look at and enjoy without feeling the work is dated.

Ismar went on to design the overall layout of the expansive park area, large central features, and public mausoleum complexes. Comprising tens of thousands of crypts, the mausoleum complexes were planned for development over many years.

Before each building season, Ismar refined the overall plan, giving detailed attention to the section designated for that year's construction. Each of the atriums, chapels and gardens has its own shape and decorative elements—skylights, railings, fountains and what Ismar called "the raisins in the cake," stone murals combining calligraphic quotations and illustrations. The wall-sized scale of the "raisins" suited him and he was pleased with the personal and decorative statements they enabled him to make. As he did for other clients, Ismar provided Pinelawn with brochures, advertising, stationery, ownership diagrams and posters in addition to architectural design. He came to see Pinelawn as "not only a resting place but a place of comfort and delight for the living." Together, the Locke family and Ismar forged a relationship that lasted more than thirty years.

In 1969, when Ismar had studio space in the Wall Street area, he began a consulting arrangement with Geyer Studio, one of a handful of New York firms offering calligraphic and engrossing services. Until late 1986, he designed many projects for Geyer, running the gamut of commercial applications for calligraphy, including scrolls, certificates, presentations and advertising. At the request of Harold Yardlan, Geyer's proprietor, Ismar conducted workshops for studio employees and once again had the pleasure of working with students.

The association with Geyer Studio, coupled with his own studies and experience as a teacher, resulted in the publication of *Our Calligraphic Heritage,* Ismar's definitive work on Roman calligraphy, issued in a limited edition by Geyer in 1979. Ismar designed a functional and decorative boxed set that contains the elements of his core beliefs about calligraphy (as expressed to his old professor years before): historical examples (study letterforms); clear, modern renderings of complete alphabets (understand them); and compositions illustrating the kind of personal application that Ismar felt was necessary artistically and viable as communication (make them your own). "It is my statement about this subject, not just another job or commercial venture," he wrote about the book. "It is my conviction that calligraphy has to be skill-oriented as well as artistic. But it also should be intimately interwoven with our cultural heritage."

To promote the book, Ismar barnstormed across the country, conducting workshops under the auspices of local calligraphic societies, often staying in the homes of members, with some of whom he maintained a lasting contact. He always hoped to make *Our Calligraphic Heritage* more widely available in a less expensive paperback edition to which end he retained the printer's film, now in the Cary Collection at RIT.

In 1984, D. Stempel AG Schriftgießerei in Frankfurt am Main contacted Ismar for permission to issue David Hebrew for use on CRTronic photo-composition systems. Ismar agreed, provided that he make the new drawings himself. David Hebrew had been copied by others many times since its original issue, with mixed or dispiriting results. Ismar said that it was possible to lift a letterform, but not the space around it, so he was glad to be able to get it right for a new generation of composition technology. On the whole, however, he was pleased to see David Hebrew become part of the cultural fabric. "I realize that a typeface design, if successful, becomes public domain," he wrote in a letter. "It becomes an image just as older styles [have], which we may admire or reject, but [which] by the nature of type [have] become the input for

ca. 1980.

other designers. I am only unhappy if, as has happened, someone lifts the design but calls it DOVID to shirk any responsibility for lifting."

In connection with his work for Stempel, Ismar traveled to Frankfurt. Various arrangements were made for him to visit colleagues and museums in the vicinity. He gave an informal talk to some art students and was chagrined to find that although he could understand what was said to him, he could no longer adequately express himself in his mother tongue. German words escaped him and a young girl stepped in to translate for him. Minor frustrations like this aside, Ismar enjoyed his trip to Germany. The changes there pleasantly astonished him: for one thing, he saw racially and ethnically diverse young people speaking German with a typical regional accent, something inconceivable in the homogeneously white society of his youth. But, he could not help but feel some of the former racial hostility from among the older generation.

After his second wife Dorothy died in 1986, Ismar moved his studio into his home, working both under his own name and with me under the name of ABCD Studio. He took vacations every year or so, and enjoyed the sights and sounds of New York City, the Sunday *New York Times* crossword puzzle, and socializing with friends. Although he suffered from its effects, Ismar made little concession to aging. He enthusiastically embraced the advice of his doctor who suggested that he exercise, but never, the doctor told him, when he was tired. Well, as Ismar told friends, the upshot was that he was *always* tired—but never, of course, too tired to work.

During the late 1980s and early 90s, Ismar remained busy with architectural work for Pinelawn, but demand for his graphic work had slowed. Undeterred, he continued to develop graphic projects. Ismar had long been aware of the lack of an adequate manual in the field of Hebrew calligraphy, and friends and students asked why he had not made a Hebrew equivalent to *Our Calligraphic Heritage*. He worked on *The Hebrew Letter: Calligraphic Variations* in between paying jobs for much of the 1980s and saw it published by Jason Aronson in 1990. Another statement of conviction and labor of love, *The Hebrew Letter* not only provides a thorough examination of Hebrew writing styles, but includes Ismar's ideas for the further development of Hebrew typography by showing several experimental type designs.

Ismar remained committed to calligraphy as a serious means of expression and devised several bilingual projects incorporating handwritten texts. In 1991 Chiswick Bookshop, Inc. published *The Book of Jonah*. Ismar worked on designs for a *Book of Ruth* and decided to fulfill a longtime ambition, designing and illustrating a Haggadah for Passover. Years earlier, Ismar had made sketches for a Haggadah project which had not gotten beyond the preliminary stages. He started fresh on *The Family Haggadah for Passover*, rethinking not only the artwork, but adapting portions of the translation as well. He did not agree with the usual rendering, "This is the Bread of Affliction . . . ," changing it to "This is the Bread of Deprivation . . . ," a wording he found more correct and meaningful.

Ismar's involvement with the 1994 renovation of the sanctuary of the Brotherhood Synagogue in New York City allowed him to explore once again some of his ideas about religious architecture and to express his affection for his heritage. Integrating into his design the spare architectural elements of the landmark building, erected in 1859 as a Friends Meeting House, Ismar set out to give the sanctuary the character of a contemporary Jewish house of worship. "To give the new ark meaning beyond the purely functional, I decided to use symbols associated with the ancient services; thus bringing past and present together. The different motives and quotations . . . had to become one composition in formal terms as well as in meaning."

The choice of text and imagery is entirely Ismar's own. Sensitive to the nuance of words, as well as their graphic impact, he paid careful attention to content. He liked the welcoming tone of the priestly blessing (Numbers 6:24–26) and featured it prominently in Hebrew and English over the Holy Ark. A telling detail in the Brotherhood Synagogue, though, is the eternal light, identified not with the customary Hebrew word meaning candle, but with the Hebrew word for the light which, in the opening passages of the *Book of Genesis,* abrogates the darkness. Aside from the continuing development of Pinelawn, this was to be Ismar's last large-scale work.

In 1995, illness finally forced Ismar to reduce his schedule, but he continued to produce, for Pinelawn and for his Haggadah, until a few weeks before his death on February 26, 1996. He is buried, surrounded by his work, in the Garden of Peace at Pinelawn Memorial Park.

In a draft for an informal talk to students, Ismar wrote, "No personal style can develop and mature in a span of a year or so. And if there is any conviction in the form of expression an artist chooses, then that conviction will stay with that artist for some time." Throughout a varied professional career that lasted more than sixty years, Ismar stayed true to his own artistic convictions. His answers to a questionnaire from a calligraphic society sum up this designer's life:

> I became interested in calligraphy when I was about sixteen years old.

> I never believed in specialization. I chose as my career the broad field of graphic and architectural design when I was in my early twenties.

> No single person [inspired me], rather admirable and outstanding work that one finds reproduced in books or hanging in museums, had its influence on my development.

> Three aspects of calligraphy are to me of equal interest and importance: study, work and teaching, in other words, to learn from historic examples, to express myself through my work, and to share my experience with others.

> Seeing other people's work may be stimulating, but I certainly would not use it as model sheets or in any other direct way.

> The most essential element [that a calligrapher needs] is the natural gift of sensitivity for form and proportion. Other important elements which the calligrapher has to supply are dedication and endurance.

On the other hand, as the wry, sly absurdist poet Christian Morgenstern wrote and Ismar liked to quote:

Und er schreibt in seine Wochenchronik, And he wrote in his diary,
Wieder ein Erlebnis voll von Honig! Another experience full of honey!

HELEN BRANDSHAFT

PLATES

Finally, I believe that in graphic art there has to be a fusion of the visual and manual. Our hands are wonderful tools. If properly trained, they can and will convey some of the artist's feeling beyond the moment in which they perform. And locked in the hand-made piece of art is some of the spiritual that we try to deliver. We do not question this in music, we should not question it in the field of visual arts.

GRAPHICS

❧ *I would consider the design of David Hebrew one of my important works. I am aware that to many that is a very esoteric matter, but to me it is an important area of self-expression. I attempted, and I hope succeeded, in fusing a sound cultural, historic foundation with a true personal, present-day expression. If I may phrase it differently, it is a process of absorbing our heritage and then creating it anew out of our own thoughts, feeling and environment.*

❧ *Skill is a great gift and it is certainly essential for any calligrapher to possess. But skill is not all. Only when it is guided by understanding and saturated with artistic personality, will it lead to worthwhile results.*

❧ I like to express through my calligraphy the belief that a graphic artist should serve the text first. Calligraphy is his tool to do so. This is very important. Every piece worthwhile writing has to be written in a way that communicates it.

Business card, ca. 1932–52.

א·דוד
ירושלים·רח׳ הקרן הקימת 8

I·DAVID
8 Hakeren Hakayemeth st.
Jerusalem · ISRAEL

Decorative binding for the Golden Book, Weizmann volume, Keren Kayemet le-Israel, Jerusalem, 1948.
"There is one way in front of us—the way of work and labor—dunim by dunim."

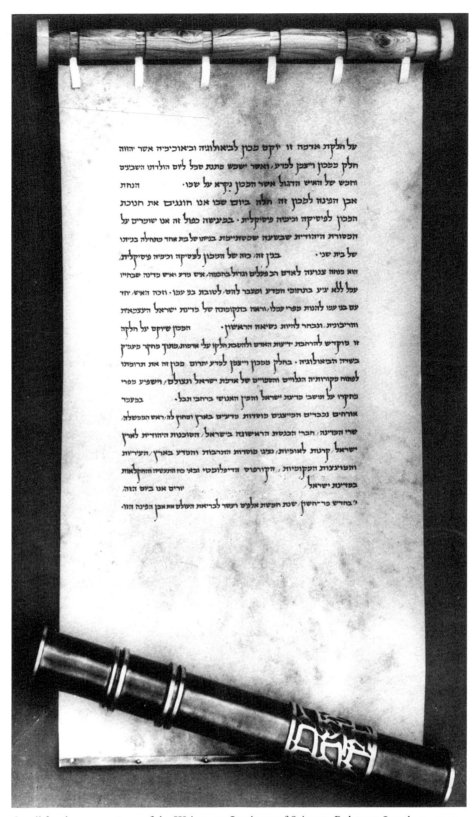

על חלקת אדמה זו יוקם מכון לביאולוגיה וביאוכימיה אשר יהווה
חלק ממכון ויצמן למדע, ואשר ישמש מתנת סבל ליום הולדתו השבעים
ונפש של האיש הדגול אשר המכון נקרא על שמו.

אבן הפנה למכון זה תלה ביום שבו אנו חוגגים את חנוכת
המכון לפיסיקה וכימיה פיסיקלית. בפעישה כפול זה אנו שומרים על
המסורת היהודיות שבשעה שמשתנימת בניינו של בת אחד מתחילה בניזו
של בית שני.   בכן זה, כזה של המכון לפסיקה וכימיה פיסיקלית,

הוא פתח צנועה לאדם רב פעלים וגדול בהמפה, איש מדע ואיש מדינה שבחייו
עמל ללא ליאע בתחומי המדע ומעבר להם, לטובת בני עמו, וזכה האיש, יחד
עם בני עמו לחזות מפרי עמלו, וראה בתקומה של מדינת ישראל העצמאית
וחריבונית, ונבחר להיות נשיאה הראשון.   המכון שיוקם על חלקה

זו פוקדיש להרחבת ידיעות האדם ולהכפבת חלקו על ארמות,מתוך פחתר פיעליק
בשדה הביאולוגיה, בחלק ממכון ויצמן למדע יתרום מכון זה את תרומתו
לפתוח מקורותיה הגלויים והספויים של ארפת ישראל ונצולם, וישפיע מפרי
מחקרו על תושבי מדינת ישראל והפין האנושי בריחבי תבל.   במעמר

אורחים נכבדים המייצגים מוסדות מדעיים בארץ ומחוץ לה, ראש הממשלה,
שרי המדינה, חברי הכנסת הראשונה בישראל, הסוכנות היהודית לארץ
ישראל, קרנות לאומיות, נציגי מוסדות הכרבוד והמדע בארץ, העיריות
והמוצרצות המקומיות, הקורפוס הדיפלומטי ובאי כת התעשיה והחקלאות
במדינת ישראל   יורדים אנו ביום הזה,

י' בחדיש פר-חשון, שנת חמשות אלפיט ועשר לבריאת העולם את אבן הפינה הזו.

Scroll for the cornerstone of the Weizmann Institute of Science, Rehovat, Israel, ca. 1949.

40

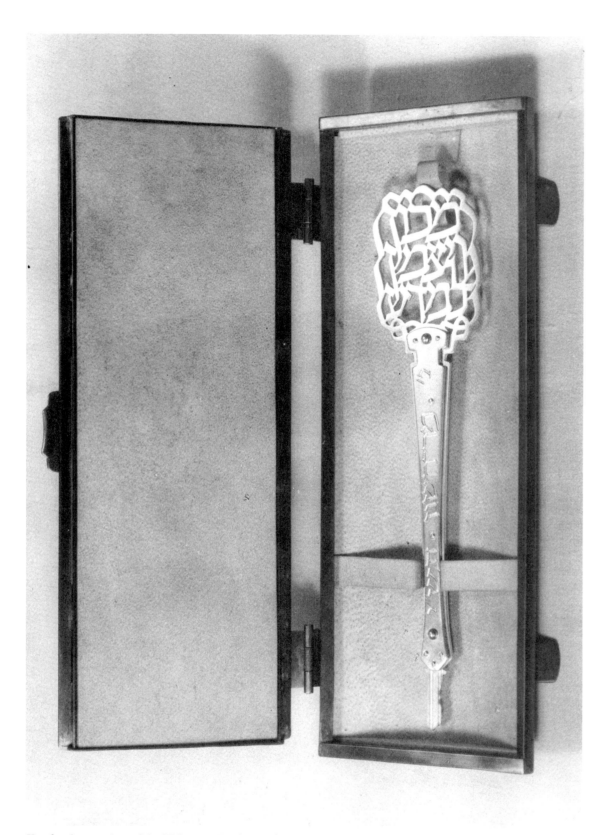

Key for the opening of the Weizmann Institute of Science, Rehovat, Israel, ca. 1949.

Jerusalem stamps for the Jewish Agency, 1948. Printed in a trial issue, but never used because of the siege of the city.

Graphics, ca. 1932–52.

Masthead for *Chronicles: News of the Past*, Jerusalem, The Reubeni Foundation, 1954.

Cigarette package designs, ca. 1932–52.

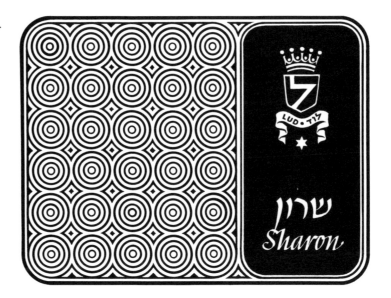

מתנות
שרלוט

charlotte's *Gifts*

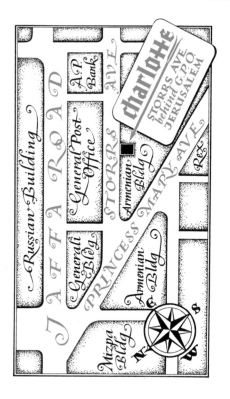

French-fold brochure for Charlotte's Gifts, [n.d.]. The logo incorporates the Hebrew letter *shin* and the Roman letter *c*, the initial letter in each language for the first name of the owner Charlotte Stern.

44

JERUSALEM AUTOMOBILE COMPANY LTD.

חברה
ירושלמית
לאוטומובילים
בע"מ

شركة سيارات القدس ليمتد

Advertisements, ca. 1932–52.

Israeli paper currency.
50 *pruta* note, 1952.

✑ *Tradition is like a thread woven into any cultural fabric. It is the inheritance that every new generation has to make its own in a revitalized and rejuvenated form until, again, younger generations take over. When we look at our present-day writing forms we can not help but sense a strange almost mystic affinity between at least some of those forms and letterforms that were written thousands of years ago. The recognition of some of these links to the past will help us to see some of the deeply rooted form principles which should remain part of letters despite the evolutionary process that, over the centuries, has altered the general appearance of writing and eventually also of printing.*

Citation for the Government of Israel, 1970. Silk screen.

46

Haganah poster no. 2, Eretz Israel, [n.d.]. Lithography. "It all depends on you."

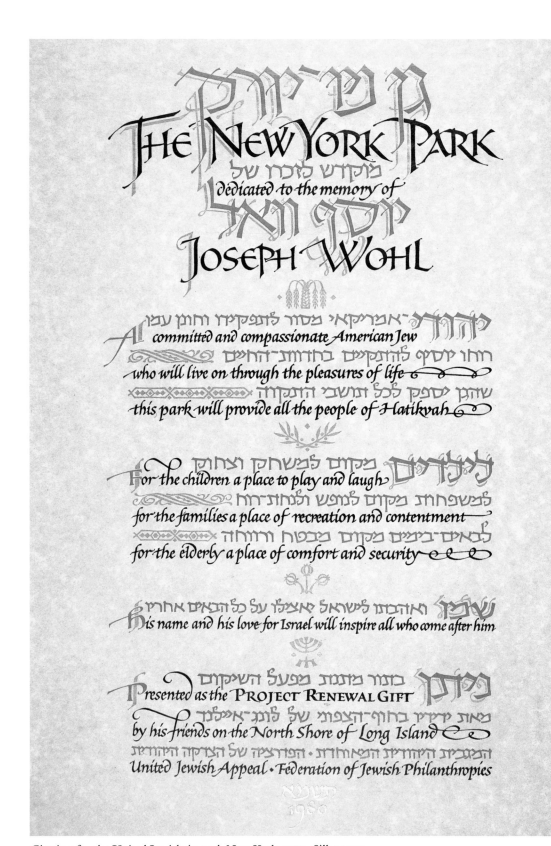

THE NEW YORK PARK

מקדש לזכר של

dedicated to the memory of

JOSEPH WOHL

יהודי־אמריקאי מסור לתפקידו וחנן עמו

A committed and compassionate American Jew

וחו ימצא להתקיים בתענות־החיים

who will live on through the pleasures of life

שהגן יספק לכל תושבי התקוה

this park will provide all the people of Hatikvah

לילדים מקום למשחק וצחוק

For the children a place to play and laugh

למשפחות מקום לנופש ותענות־רוח

for the families a place of recreation and contentment

לבאים־בימים מקום מבטח ורווחה

for the elderly a place of comfort and security

שמן ואהבתו לישראל ישצילו על כל הבאים אחרין

His name and his love for Israel will inspire all who come after him

מתן במזור מתנת מפעל השיקום

Presented as the PROJECT RENEWAL GIFT

מאת ידידיו בחוף־הצפוני של לונג־אילנד

by his friends on the North Shore of Long Island

המגבית היהודית המאוחדת · הפדרציה של הצדקה היהודית

United Jewish Appeal · Federation of Jewish Philanthropies

תשמ"א
1980

Citation for the United Jewish Appeal, New York, 1980. Silk screen.

THE NIGHTINGALE PLEDGE

I SOLEMNLY PLEDGE

myself before God and in the presence of this assembly to pass my life in purity and to practice my profession faithfully. I will abstain from whatever is deleterious and mischievous and will not take or knowingly administer any harmful drug.

I WILL DO ALL IN MY POWER

to elevate the standard of my profession, and will hold in confidence all personal matters committed to my keeping, and all family affairs coming to my knowledge in the practice of my calling.

WITH LOYALTY

will I aid the physician in his work and devote myself to the welfare of those committed to my care.

Broadside for *RN Magazine*, Oradell, NJ, 1971. Offset lithography.

FAITH HOPE AND LOVE · THESE THREE ABIDE · BUT THE GREATEST OF THESE IS LOVE

ST. PAUL OF TARSUS

Broadside for Pinelawn Memorial Park, Farmingdale, NY, 1971. Offset lithography.

50

Pages for the Society of Scribes calendar, New York, 1977. Offset lithography.

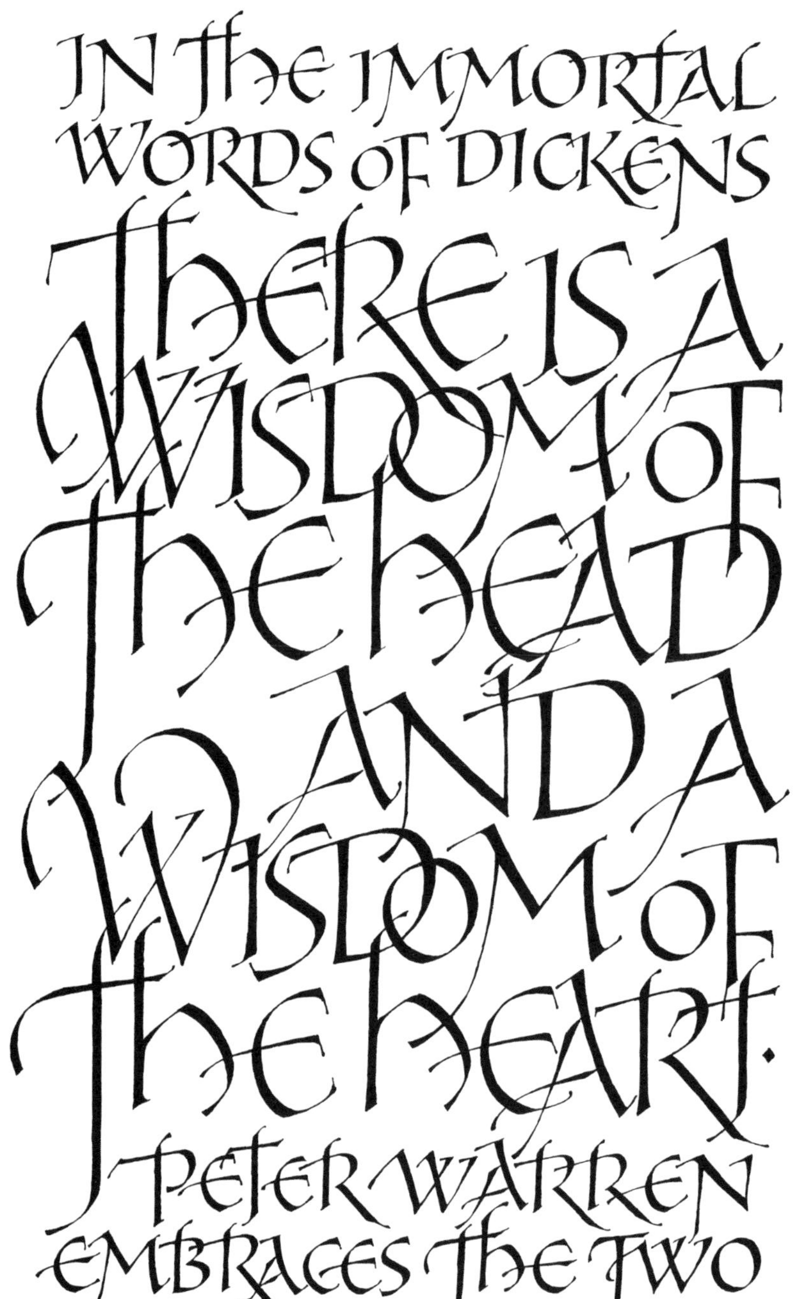

IN THE IMMORTAL
WORDS OF DICKENS
THERE IS A
WISDOM OF
THE HEAD
AND A
WISDOM OF
THE HEART.
PETER WARREN
EMBRACES THE TWO

Design for etched metal plate,
used as centerpiece in citation
for PepsiCo, Inc., and Pepsi-
Cola, International, Purchase,
NY, 1985.

The Bibliophiles

Logo for The Bibliophiles, 1971.

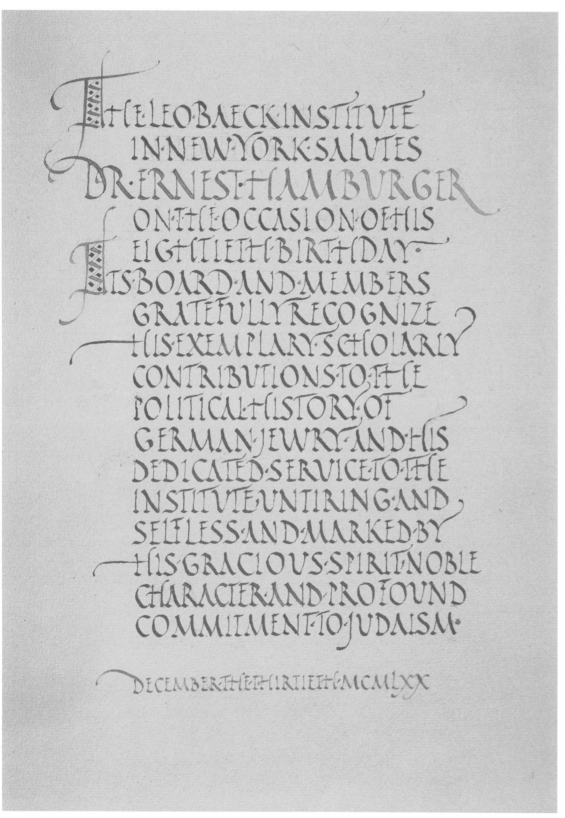

THE LEO BAECK INSTITUTE
IN NEW YORK SALUTES
DR. ERNEST HAMBURGER
ON THE OCCASION OF HIS
EIGHTIETH BIRTHDAY.
ITS BOARD AND MEMBERS
GRATEFULLY RECOGNIZE
HIS EXEMPLARY SCHOLARLY
CONTRIBUTIONS TO THE
POLITICAL HISTORY OF
GERMAN JEWRY AND HIS
DEDICATED SERVICE TO THE
INSTITUTE UNTIRING AND
SELFLESS AND MARKED BY
HIS GRACIOUS SPIRIT NOBLE
CHARACTER AND PROFOUND
COMMITMENT TO JUDAISM.

DECEMBER THE THIRTIETH MCMLXX

Draft of citation for Leo Baeck Institute, New York, 1970. Gouache.

53

Poster for Jewish Book Council of America, New York, 1968. Offset lithography.

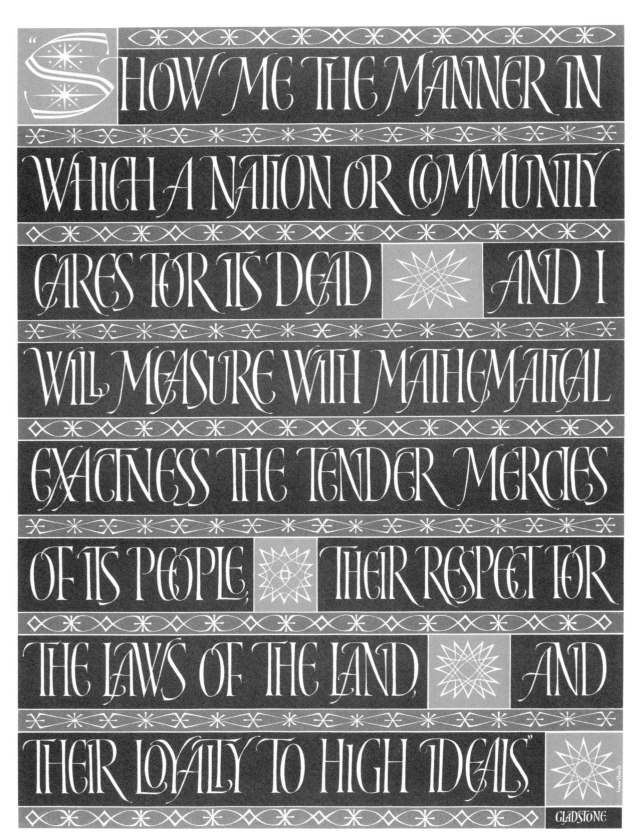

"Show me the manner in which a nation or community cares for its dead and I will measure with mathematical exactness the tender mercies of its people, their respect for the laws of the land, and their loyalty to high ideals."

GLADSTONE

Poster for Pinelawn Memorial Park, Farmingdale, NY, 1977. Offset lithography.

TRUTH AND REASON MAY
APPEAR TO BE CRUSHED,
BUT IN OUR HEARTS THEY
REMAIN ETERNALLY FREE,
AND FROM THE SERENE
HEIGHTS OF ART THE
INTELLECT MAY LAUGH AT
THE TRIUMPH OF FOLLY…
SECURE IN THE BOND
RELATING IT TO ALL THAT IS
BEST ON EARTH. DIESER FRIEDE
. THOMAS MANN

ALL THAT IS BEST ON EARTH FROM THE DIRECTORS OF THE LIMITED EDITIONS CLUB

Calligraphic drawing by Ismar David, printed on Italian mould-made paper and colored by hand

Broadside holiday greeting from the Limited Editions Club, New York, 1969. Offset lithography.

Poster, 1976. Silk screen. The artist supervised the mixing of the inks in order to create the blend of overprinted colors.

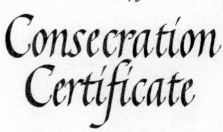

בֹּא בְּרוּךְ יְהוָה

ENTER·THOU·BLESSED·OF·THE·LORD

GENESIS, 24:31

Consecration
Certificate

THIS IS TO RECORD THAT

_____

WAS CONSECRATED

ON THE_____DAY OF_____19___

CORRESPOND-
ING TO THE_____DAY OF_____57___

AT CONGREGATION _____

_____

AND ENROLLED AS A STUDENT IN
ITS RELIGIOUS SCHOOL

_____
RABBI

_____
SIGNATURE

_____
SIGNATURE

TRAIN·UP·A·CHILD·IN·THE·WAY·HE·SHOULD·GO·
AND·EVEN·WHEN·HE·IS·OLD·HE·WILL·
NOT·DEPART·FROM·IT·

PROV. 22: 6

Certificate for the Union of American Hebrew Congregations, New York, 1964. Offset lithography.

58

PRAISED
BE THOU
O LORD
OUR GOD
RULER
OF THE
UNIVERSE
WHO HAS
SANCTIFIED
US BY THY
COMMAND
MENTS
AND
ORDAINED
THAT
WE SHALL
ENTER
OUR SON
INTO THE
COVENANT
OF
ABRAHAM
OUR
FATHER

B'RIS MILAH CERTIFICATE

In conformity with the hallowed observance of the Jewish faith

_____

son of_____

and_____

was brought into the covenant of Abraham and given the Hebrew name

of_____

_____

at_____

_____

DATE OF BIRTH _____ 19 __

_____ 57 __

_____
SIGNATURE

_____
SIGNATURE

_____
SIGNATURE

MAY THIS
COVENANT
BE
FULFILLED
IN HIM
BY
DEVOTION
TO THY
LAW OF
TRUTH
AND
RIGHTEOUS
NESS
BY A
MARRIAGE
WORTHY
OF THY
BLESSING
AND BY
A LIFE
ENRICHED
WITH
GOOD
DEEDS

Certificate for the Union of American Hebrew Congregations, New York, 1964. Offset lithography.

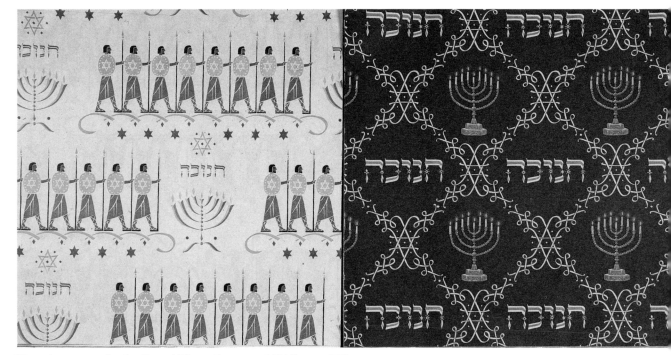

Wrapping papers for the Crystal Tissue Company, Middleton, OH, 1955.

Personal greeting card, 1958. Letterpress.

60

Greeting card, [n.d.]. Silk screen.

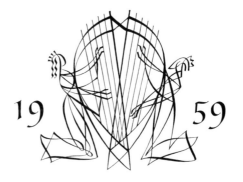

Greeting card, 1959. Letterpress.

Announcement, 1975–76. Offset lithography.

Mr. and Mrs. Albert A. List
Mr. and Mrs. Joseph M. Zelman
request the honor of your presence
at the marriage of their children
VIKI AND NOAM
on Saturday evening, the thirteenth
of May at half after eight o'clock
Byram Shore Road
Byram, Connecticut

Kindly respond

שמחו. בשיר. בחודה. ובחולות. ורקים
הננו
מתכבדים להזמין
את כבודכם להשתתף
בשמחת כלולת בננו היקרים
הבחור החתן נעם דבני *
עם בחירת לבו
הכלה המעלה
ורדה זתי

הורי החתן יוסף מאיר זעלמן ורעיתו מתיה
הורי הכלה אברהם ליסט ורעיתו דבורה

62

1

2

3

4

5

6

7

8

9

10

11

12

Trademarks:

1. World Council of Synagogues, 1961.
2. Riverside Studies in Literature, [n.d.].
3. Bell Telephone Laboratories, 1960.
4. Brotherhood Synagogue, [n.d.].
5. Geyer Studio, [n.d.].
6. Houghton MiZ in History, 1964.
7 & 8. World Trade Institute, 1971.
9. Golden Press, [n.d.].
10. Riverside Editions, 1964.
11. Fleming H. Revell Company, 1962.
12. For Harper & Row Publishers.

63

Acrostic passage from Proverbs 31:10–31. The initial letters form the *alephbet*.

64

דוד

David Hebrew

✍ *But of course all technical aspects had to be considered within the framework of Western achievements in typographical design. I intended to go one step further in the conception of a type family and add a sans serif to a text face and an oblique, and I developed these three variations from one basic form conception, rendering each variation in three weights. Each letter of these nine variations would fit on the same matrix and line up in print on the same baseline. This is always a problem that goes with designs intended for the line-casting machines. In those days no one in Palestine thought of anything else. I had to come to grips also with proportions of letters and devised a division of the alphabet into three groups: one group of narrow letters, then a group of medium width that included all letters with only one vertical element with a very few others, and a third, wide group including most letters with two full vertical elements or more. This system brought a much higher degree of evenness in structure and texture than is usual in Hebrew typography which too often suffers from spottiness.*

עפצקרשתדסוןץ

עפצקרשתדסוןץ

עפצקרשתדסוןץ

עפצקרשתדסוןץ

עפצקרשתדסוןץ

עפצקרשתדסוןץ

עפצקרשתדסוןץ

עפצקרשתדסוןץ

עפצקרשתדסוןץ

David Hebrew, issued by Intertype in 1954 in a family of three variations and three weights. In the early to mid-193⟨
Ismar David began thinking about a family of book, cursive and sans serif types, each in three weights. Between 19⟨
and 1950 he developed the preliminary versions of his conception. After signing a contract with Intertype Corporatio⟨
in 1951, he made the final renderings which he delivered in 1952. David's contribution to the typographic portfolio *Lib⟨*
Librorum (1955) was the first international showing of the new typeface. The book designer Moshe Spitzer chose the fa⟨
for Shmuel Joseph Agnon's *A Stray Dog* (1960), the first complete book to be printed in David Hebrew.

אבגדהוזחטיכלמנ

אבגדהוזחטיכלמנ

אבגדהוזחטיכלמנ

אבגדהוזחטיכלמנ

אבגדהוזחטיכלמנ

אבגדהוזחטיכלמנ

אבגדהוזחטיכלמנ

אבגדהוזחטיכלמנ

אבגדהוזחטיכלמנ

From the start I had planned these alphabets for slug composition. Monotype equipment, at that time, was not in operation in Palestine and it seemed unlikely that it would be introduced in the foreseeable future. My dream was to enable every printer in the country to produce well planned and well organized printing for books and commerce, aesthetically comparable to printing with Roman type. . . . My dream of the large family, including a sans serif never materialized; the full scheme is shown only in an essay about Hebrew typefaces by Dr. Spitzer for the Schoken-Festschrift.

12 Point David Hebrew with Italic

אני חבצלת השרון שושנת העמקים: כשושנה בין
החוחים כן רעיתי בין הבנות: כתפוח בעצי היער
כן דודי בין הבנים בצלו חמדתי וישבתי ופריו מתוק
לחכי: הביאני אל־בית היין ודגלו עלי אהבה:
סמכוני באשישות רפדוני בתפוחים כי־חולת אהבה
אני: שמאלו תחת לראשי וימינו תחבקני: השבעתי
אתכם בנות ירושלם בצבאות או באילות השדה
אם־תעירו ואם־תעוררו את־האהבה עד שתחפץ:
קול דודי הנה־זה בא מדלג על־ההרים מקפץ על־
הגבעות: דומה דודי לצבי או לעפר האילים הנה־
זה עומד אחר כתלנו משגיח מן־החלנות מציץ מן־
החרכים: ענה דודי ואמר לי קומי לך רעיתי יפתי
ולכי־לך: כי־הנה הסתו עבר הגשם חלף הלך לו:
הנצנים נראו בארץ עת הזמיר הגיע וקול התור
נשמע בארצנו: התאנה חנטה פגיה והגפנים סמדר
נתנו ריח קומי לכי רעיתי יפתי ולכי־לך: יונתי
בחגוי הסלע בסתר המדרגה הראיני את־מראיך
השמיעני את־קולך כי־קולך ערב ומראיך נאוה:
אחזו־לנו שעלים שעלים קטנים מחבלים כרמים
וכרמינו סמדר: דודי לי ואני לו הרעה בשושנים:
עד שיפוח היום ונסו הצללים סב דמה־לך דודי
לצבי או לעפר האילים על־הרי בתר:

(set solid)

אני חבצלת השרון
שושנת העמקים:
כשושנה בין החוחים
כן רעיתי בין הבנות:
כתפוח בעצי היער
כן דודי בין הבנים
בצלו חמדתי וישבתי
ופריו מתוק לחכי:
הביאני אל־בית היין
ודגלו עלי אהבה:
סמכוני באשישות
רפדוני בתפוחים
כי־חולת אהבה אני:
שמאלו תחת לראשי
וימינו תחבקני:
השבעתי אתכם בנות ירושלם
בצבאות או באילות השדה
אם־תעירו ואם־תעוררו

(two point leaded)

אני חבצלת השרון
שושנת העמקיס:
כשושנה בין החוחיס
כן רעיתי בין הבנות:
כתפוח בעצי היער
כן דודי בין הבניס
בצלו חמדתי וישבתי
ופריו מתוק לחכי:
הביאני אל־בית היין
ודגלו עלי אהבה:
סמכוני באשישות
רפדוני בתפוחיס
כי־חולת אהבה אני:
שמאלו תחת לראשי
וימינו תחבקני:
השבעתי אתכס בנות ירושלס
בצבאות או באילות השזה
אס־תעירו ואס־תעוררו

(two point leaded)

Proof of David Hebrew, Intertype Corporation, Brooklyn, 1954.

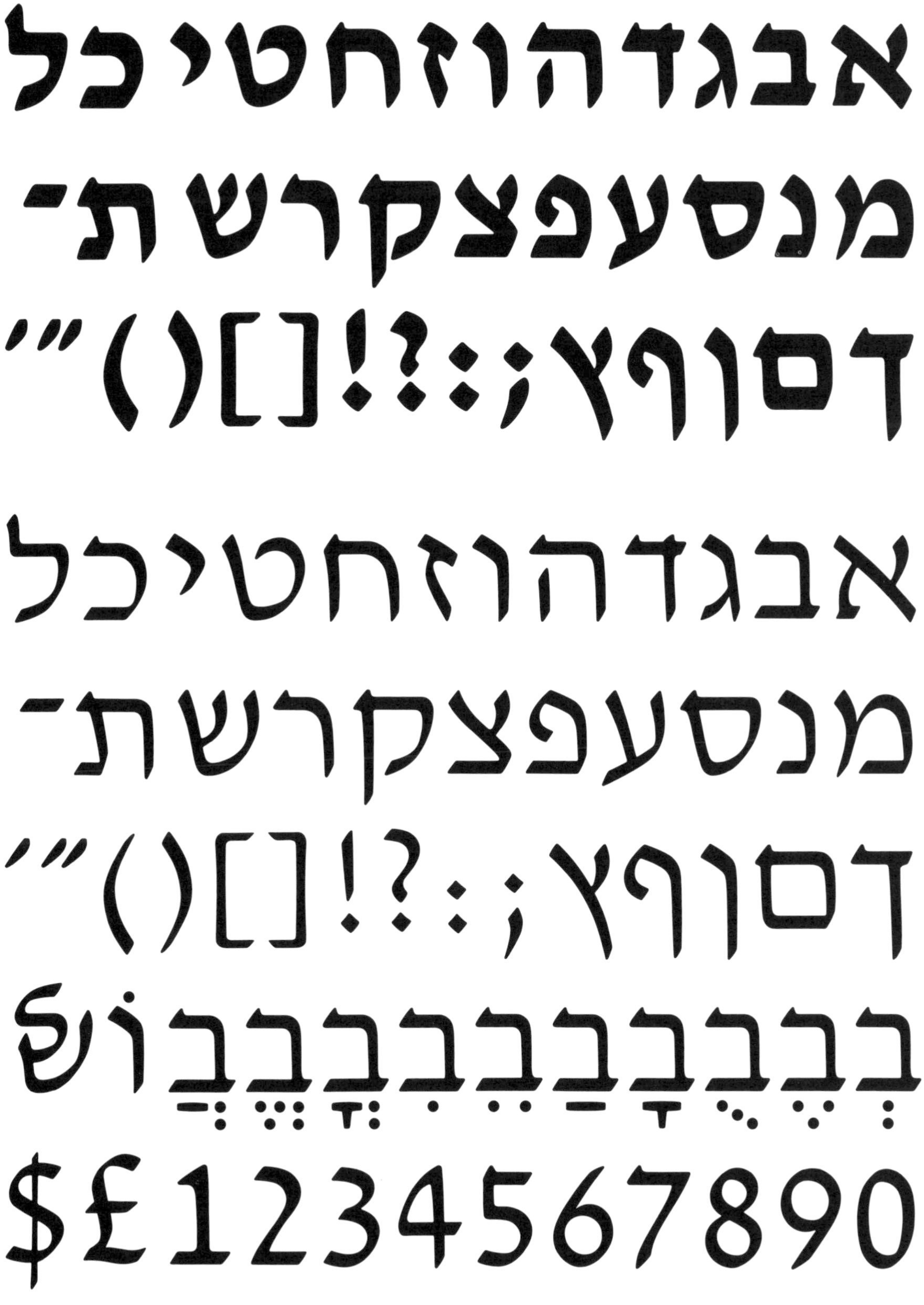

אבגדהוזחטיכל
מנסעפצקרשת־
’”()[]!?:;ךץףן
דסוףץ

אבגדהוזחטיכל
מנסעפצקרשת־
’”()[]!?:;ךץףן
דסוףץ

בְּבַּבָּבֵבְּבֶבֻבֹּשֻׁוֹשֻׁ

$£1234567890

Two weights of David Hebrew redrawn at the request of D. Stempel AG Schriftgießerei, Frankfurt am Main, for Linotype electronic composition systems, 1984. Drawings include a design for a shekel symbol.

א‎ב‎ג‎ד‎ה‎ו‎ז‎ח‎ט‎י‎כ‎ל‎מ‎נ‎ס‎ :

ע‎פ‎צ‎ק‎ר‎ש‎ת‎ר‎ו‎ם‎ף‎ ז‎ ??!!.

Siddur typeface for Photolettering, Inc., New York. The large decorative letters were designed as a display face for *The Traditional Prayer Book*, Springfield, NJ, Behrman House, 1963.

abcdefghijklmn

opqurstvwxyz?;;:

ABCDEFGHJKL!)

MNPQURSTVW

XYZ-"123456789

Inscripta typeface for Photolettering, Inc., New York, [n.d.].

ABCDEFGHIJ
JKLMNOPQ!
RSTUVWXYZ
$1234567890
abcdefghijkl
mnopqrstuv
wxyz-"&()?:;"
1234567890

David Classic typeface for Photolettering, Inc., New York, [n.d.].

hamburgefonstiv
HAMBURGEFONSTIV

hamburgefonstiv
HAMBURGEFONSTIV

hamburgefonstiv
HAMBURGEFONSTIV

hamburgefonstiv
HAMBURGEFONSTIV

hamburgefonstiv
HAMBURGEFONSTIV

hamburgefonstiv
HAMBURGEFONSTIV

Type design in six variants and two weights (not issued), 1992.

ABCDEFGHI
JKLMNOPR
STUVWXYZ

Alphabet designed for *Jericho: The South Beheld,* Birmingham, AL, Oxmoor House, 1974.

ABCDEFGHIJ
KLMNPQUR
STVWXYZ
1234567890

Alphabet design, [n.d.].

בְּרֵאשִׁית שְׁמוֹת וַיִּקְרָא בְּמִדְבַּר דְּבָרִים

ספר ראשון ספר שני ספר
ספר רביעי ספר חמישי

Hebrew display lettering, 1973. The large display letters appear in several books published by the Union of American Hebrew Congregations, New York.

וןיגזנחהתמש וןיגזנחהתמש וןיגזנחהתמש
ךרכבלעפצץ1 ךרכבלעפצץ1 ךרכבלעפצץ1
טקאסם?!;"ָ טקאסם?!;"ָ טקאסם?!;"ָ
798645230 798645230 798645230
תהלימספר **תהלימספר** **תהלימספר**
תהלימספר **תהלימספר** **תהלימספר**
תהלימספר תהלימספר תהלימספר

וןיגזנחהתמש וןיגזנחהתמש וןיגזנחהתמש
ךרכבלעפצץ1 ךרכבלעפצץ1 ךרכבלעפצץ1
טקאסם?!;"ָ טקאסם?!;"ָ טקאסם?!;"ָ
798645230 798645230 798645230
תהלימספר **תהלימספר** **תהלימספר**
תהלימספר **תהלימספר** **תהלימספר**
תהלימספר תהלימספר תהלימספר

וןיגזנחהתמש וןיגזנחהתמש וןיגזנחהתמש
ךרכבלעפצץ1 ךרכבלעפצץ1 ךרכבלעפצץ1
טקאסם?!;"ָ טקאסם?!;"ָ טקאסם?!;"ָ
798645230 798645230 798645230
תהלימספר **תהלימספר** **תהלימספר**
תהלימספר **תהלימספר** **תהלימספר**
תהלימספר תהלימספר תהלימספר

וןיגזנחהתמש וןיגזנחהתמש וןיגזנחהתמש
ךרכבלעפצץ1 ךרכבלעפצץ1 ךרכבלעפצץ1
טקאסם?!;"ָ טקאסם?!;"ָ טקאסם?!;"ָ
798645230 798645230 798645230
תהלימספר **תהלימספר** **תהלימספר**
תהלימספר **תהלימספר** **תהלימספר**
תהלימספר תהלימספר תהלימספר

Hebrew san-serif design in four weights, [n.d.].

ABCDE
FGHIJK
LMNOP
QRSTU
VWXYZ

Calligraphic square capital alphabet, [n.d.].

ABCDEFG
HIJKLMN
OPQRSTU
VWXYZ!?

AERW

Calligraphic uncial alphabet with alternate forms, [n.d.].

BOOK WORK

꙳ Today we are flooded with styles. Most, of course, are acceptable only in contexts relating to the past and are considered irrelevant to the present. The present styles are few and short-lived. In fact, style has taken on the meaning of fashion. Each style, of course, is valid if genuine, but for any artist it is painful to watch how some works are praised in one season only to be discarded in the next. No personal style can develop and mature in a span of a year or so. And if there is any conviction in the form of expression an artist chooses, then that conviction will stay with that artist for some time.

꙳ Of course I also like to use color. But here, too, I will not use it in a realistic fashion. Color can create texture and background. It can create tension. And if used successfully, it will complement or support my lines and strengthen their impact. So I use lines and color, but mainly lines, not in the framework of -isms like realism, expressionism or impressionism, but to serve my own needs and to communicate my ideas and my feelings in the service of the book.

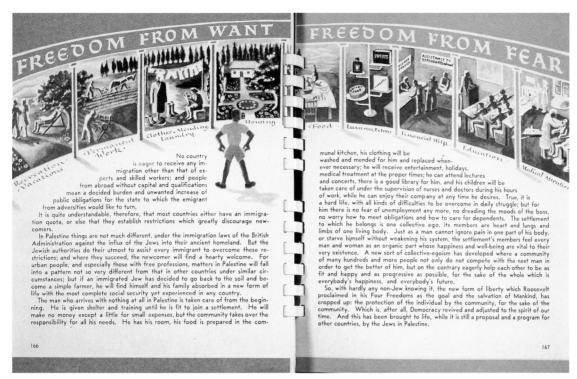

Double-page spread from *Promised Land*, E. K. Thorbecke, New York, Harper, 1947.

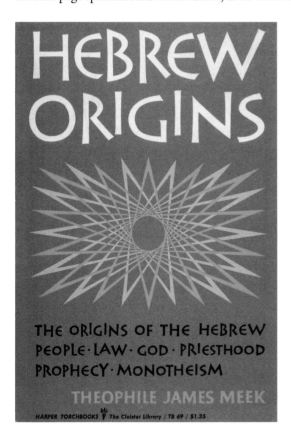

Paperback cover for *Hebrew Origins,* New York,
Harper, 1960.

Dust jacket for *The Beatitudes,* Westwood, NJ,
Fleming H. Revell, 1967.

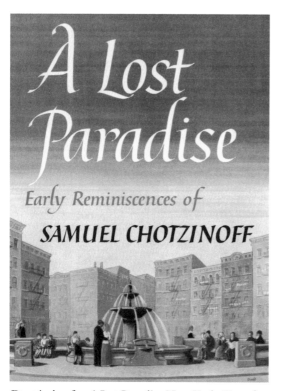

Dust jacket for *A Lost Paradise,* New York, Knopf, 1955.

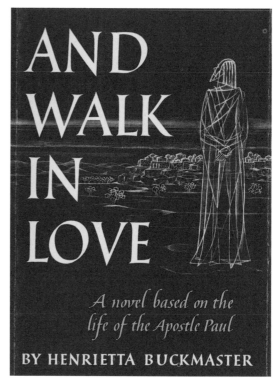

Dust jacket for *And Walk In Love,* New York, Random House, 1956.

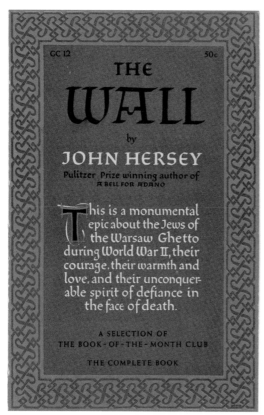

Paperback cover for *The Wall,* New York, Pocket Books, 1954.

Dust jacket for *Metamorphoses,* Bloomington, Indiana University Press, 1955.

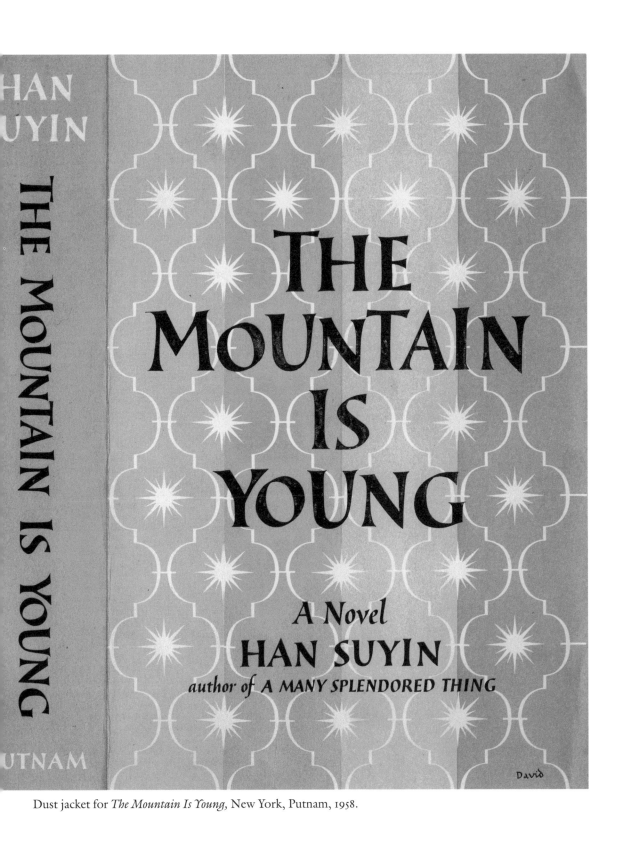

Dust jacket for *The Mountain Is Young,* New York, Putnam, 1958.

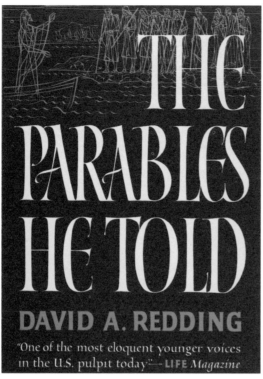

Dust jacket for *The Parables He Told,* Westwood, NJ, Fleming H. Revell, 1962.

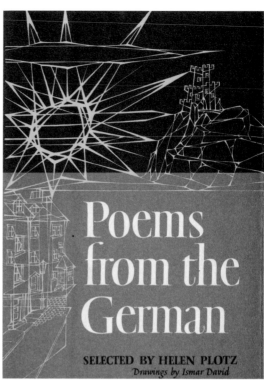

Dust jacket for *Poems from the German,* New York, Crowell, 1967.

Dust jacket for *Tongue of Flame,* New York, Crowell, 1967.

Dust jacket for *Southerner,* Philadelphia, Lippincott, 1966.

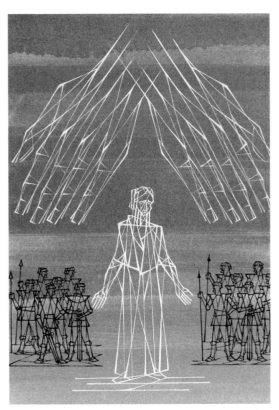

Illustration for *The Beatitudes: An Interpretation,* by C. L. Allen, Westwood, NJ, Fleming H. Revell, 1967.

Illustration for *The Beatitudes: An Interpretation,* by C. L. Allen, Westwood, NJ, Fleming H. Revell, 1967.

Illustration for *The Ten Commandments: An Interpretation,* by C. L. Allen, Westwood, NJ, Fleming H. Revell, 1965.

Illustration for *The Lord's Prayer: An Interpretation,* by C. L. Allen, Westwood, NJ, Fleming H. Revell, 1967.

HAYYIM SCHAUSS

The Lifetime of a Jew

throughout the ages
of Jewish History

Paperback cover for *The Lifetime of a Jew,* New York, Union of American Hebrew Congregations, 1976.

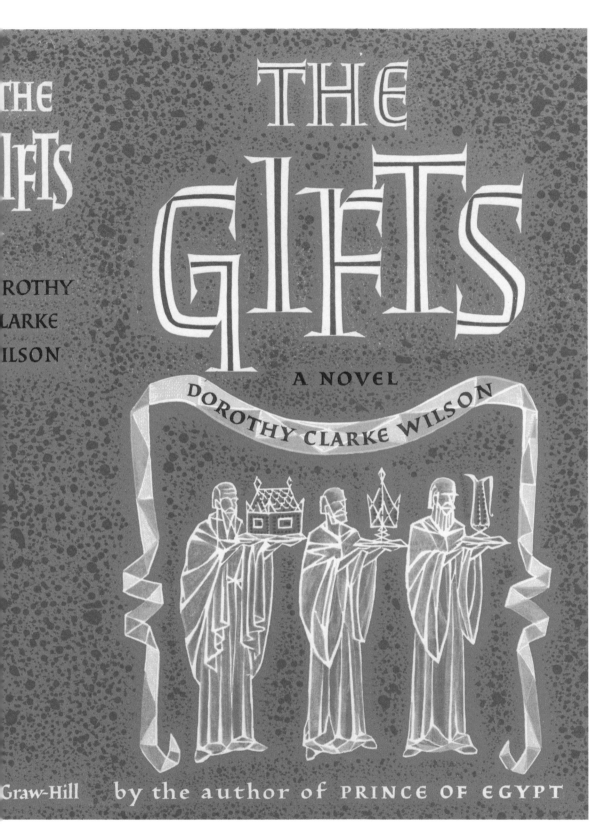

Dust jacket for *The Gifts: A Story of the Boyhood of Jesus*, New York, McGraw-Hill, 1957.

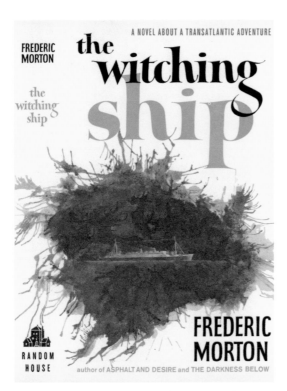

Dust jacket for *The Witching Ship,* New York, Random House, 1960.

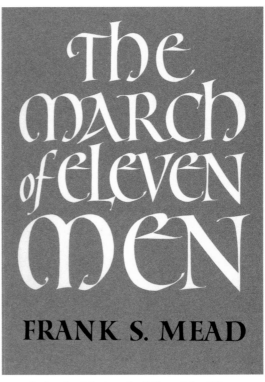

Dust jacket for *The March of Eleven Men,* Westwood, NJ, Fleming H. Revell, 1960.

Dust jacket for *War of Amazing Love,* Westwood, NJ, Fleming H. Revell, 1965.

Dust jacket for *V.,* Philadelphia, Lippincott, 1963.

88

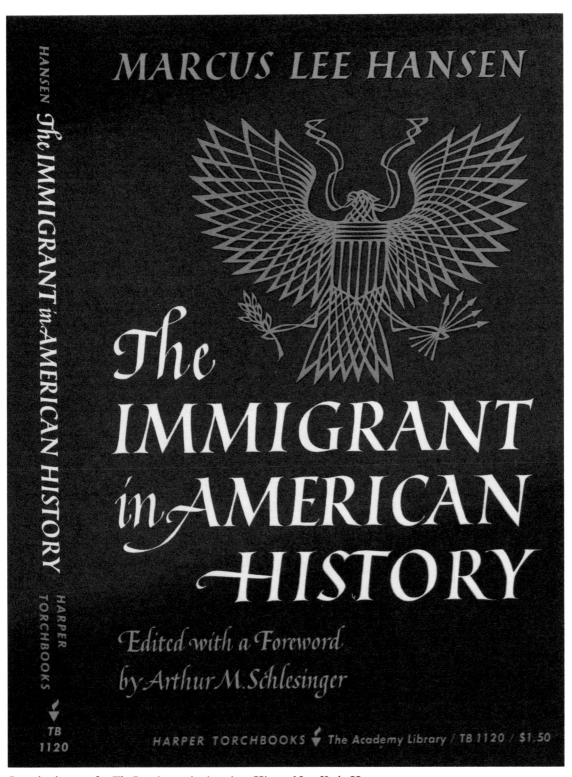

Paperback cover for *The Immigrant in American History*, New York, Harper, 1964.

"Shepherd and Fighter," illustration for *Les Pensées*, New York, The Limited Editions Club, 1971.
From "The Artist's Notes": *Pascal was a fighter during his short life. Looking up to Christ, his ideal, he saw in him not just the shepherd of the flock but the great fighter against untruth and evil.*

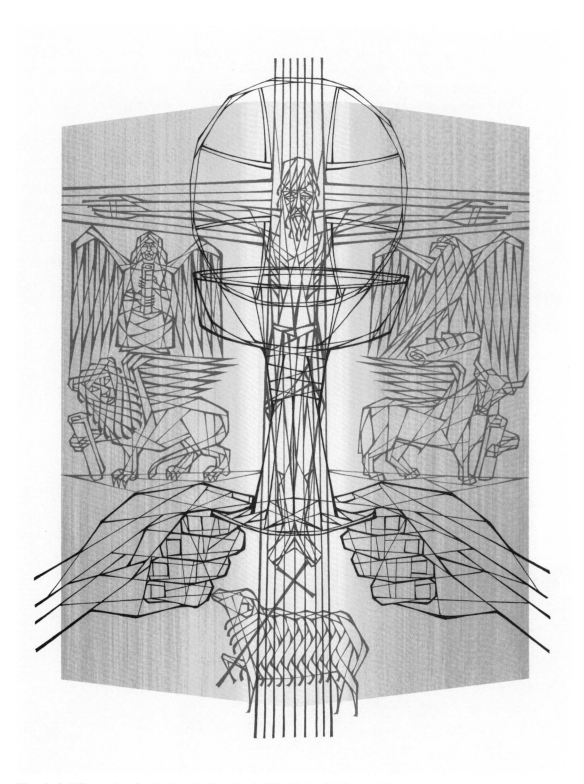

"Symbols," illustration for *Les Pensées,* New York, The Limited Editions Club, 1971.
From "The Artist's Notes": *Pascal stresses that the scriptures contain many parables, symbolic passages with hidden meanings. But symbols – such as those of Catholicism depicted here – should not just be seen and recognized; they should rather remind us of what they stand for.*

The style in which the compositions of THE PSALMS are drawn is not accidental; it rather reflects a very personal attitude towards art and design. It is the result of the gradual development and refining of a form of graphics in which I started many years ago. I came to believe that specifically religious art should not be confining but suggestive instead, stimulating the imagination of the viewer. The compositions of THE PSALMS, therefore, are more of a stage setting or background but are not illustrations in the conventional sense.

To achieve this, emphasis is on the symbolic. Does not art have to be symbolic to rise above the plain factual? I learned to admire this symbolism from the old Far Eastern art, where everything is expressed symbolically. But the symbol is only successful when it evokes the atmosphere, feeling or spirit of the subject chosen by the artist. I also have been fascinated by the greatest symbols we the human race have created: the letter forms of our alphabets. Specifically, how their lines have ceased completely to define areas or forms and have developed a life of their own. In my compositions, these lines may be light or heavy, swelling or diminishing, straight or curved. Certain lines may dominate while others may play a supporting role. The patterns and textures they finally form are to become the specific symbols, pure and transparent in their abstract harmony but aimed to convey, above all, the Psalmist's poetry. This art makes its immediate appeal to the eye, as visual art should. But through the eye it has to reach the mind of the viewer and make it respond.

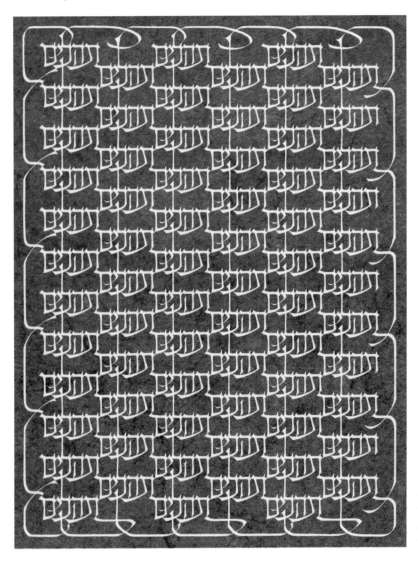

Endpaper for *The Psalms*, New York, Union of American Hebrew Congregations, 1973.

92

תהלים
the
psalms

A LIMITED EDITION
of the new English translation prepared by
the Jewish Publication Society of America
issued on the occasion
of the one-hundredth anniversary of the
Union of American Hebrew Congregations
with drawings by Ismar David

THE UNION OF
AMERICAN HEBREW CONGREGATIONS
NEW YORK 1973-תשל״ג

Prospectus for *The Psalms,* New York, Union of American Hebrew Congregations, 1973.

145

תהלה לדוד	1	A song of praise; of David.

אֲרוֹמִמְךָ אֱלוֹהַי הַמֶּלֶךְ
וַאֲבָרְכָה שִׁמְךָ לְעוֹלָם וָעֶד:

I will extol You, my God and king,
   and bless Your name forever and ever.

בְּכָל־יוֹם אֲבָרְכֶךָּ
וַאֲהַלְלָה שִׁמְךָ לְעוֹלָם וָעֶד:

2 Every day will I bless You
   and praise Your name forever and ever.

גָּדוֹל יְהוָה וּמְהֻלָּל מְאֹד
וְלִגְדֻלָּתוֹ אֵין חֵקֶר:

3 Great is the Lᴏʀᴅ and much acclaimed;
   His greatness cannot be fathomed.

דּוֹר לְדוֹר יְשַׁבַּח מַעֲשֶׂיךָ
וּגְבוּרֹתֶיךָ יַגִּידוּ:

4 One generation shall laud Your works to another
   and declare Your mighty acts.

הֲדַר כְּבוֹד הוֹדֶךָ
וְדִבְרֵי נִפְלְאֹתֶיךָ אָשִׂיחָה:

5 The glorious majesty of Your splendor
   and Your wondrous acts will I recite.

וֶעֱזוּז נוֹרְאֹתֶיךָ יֹאמֵרוּ
וּגְדוּלָּתְךָ אֲסַפְּרֶנָּה:

6 Men shall talk of the might of Your awesome deeds,
   and I will recount Your greatness.

זֵכֶר רַב־טוּבְךָ יַבִּיעוּ
וְצִדְקָתְךָ יְרַנֵּנוּ:

7 They shall celebrate Your abundant goodness,
   and sing joyously of Your beneficence.

חַנּוּן וְרַחוּם יְהוָה
אֶרֶךְ אַפַּיִם וּגְדָל־חָסֶד:

8 The Lᴏʀᴅ is gracious and compassionate,
   slow to anger and abounding in kindness.

טוֹב־יְהוָה לַכֹּל
וְרַחֲמָיו עַל־כָּל־מַעֲשָׂיו:

9 The Lᴏʀᴅ is good to all,
   and His mercy is upon all His works.

יוֹדוּךָ יְהוָה כָּל־מַעֲשֶׂיךָ
וַחֲסִידֶיךָ יְבָרְכוּכָה:

10 All Your works shall praise You, O Lᴏʀᴅ,
   and Your faithful ones shall bless You.

Double-page spread from *The Psalms*, New York, Union of American Hebrew Congregations, 1973.

	11 They shall talk of the majesty of Your kingship,
כבוד מלכותך יאמרו	and speak of Your might,
וגבורתך ידברו:	
להודיע לבני האדם גבורתיו	12 to make His mighty acts known among men
וכבוד הדר מלכותו:	and the majestic glory of His kingship.
מלכותך מלכות כל־עלמים	13 Your kingship is an eternal kingship;
וממשלתך בכל־דור ודר:	Your dominion is for all generations.
סומך יהוה לכל־הנפלים	14 The LORD supports all who stumble,
וזוקף לכל־הכפופים:	and makes all who are bent stand straight.
עיני־כל אליך ישברו	15 The eyes of all look to You expectantly,
ואתה נותן־להם את־אכלם בעתו:	and You give them their food when it is due.
פותח את־ידך	16 You give it openhandedly,
ומשביע לכל־חי רצון:	feeding every creature to its heart's content.
צדיק יהוה בכל־דרכיו	17 The LORD is beneficent in all His ways
וחסיד בכל־מעשיו:	and faithful in all His works.
קרוב יהוה לכל־קראיו	18 The LORD is near to all who call Him,
לכל אשר יקראהו באמת:	to all who call Him with sincerity.
רצון־יראיו יעשה	19 He fulfills the wishes of those who fear Him;
ואת־שועתם ישמע ויושיעם:	He hears their cry and delivers them.
שומר יהוה את־כל־אהביו	20 The LORD watches over all who love Him,
ואת כל־הרשעים ישמיד:	but all the wicked will He destroy.
תהלת יהוה ידבר־פי	21 My mouth shall utter the praise of the LORD,
ויברך כל־בשר שם קדשו לעולם ועד:	and all creatures*a* shall bless His holy name forever and ever.

a Lit. "flesh"

146

הללו־יה	1 Hallelujah.
הללי נפשי את־יהוה:	Praise the LORD, O my soul!
אהללה יהוה בחיי	2 I will praise the LORD all my life,
אזמרה לאלהי בעודי:	sing hymns to my God while I exist.
אל־תבטחו בנדיבים	3 Put not your trust in the great,
בבן־אדם שאין לו תשועה:	in mortal man who cannot save.
תצא רוחו	4 His breath departs;
ישב לאדמתו	he returns to the dust;
ביום ההוא אבדו עשתנתיו:	on that day his plans come to nothing.
אשרי שאל יעקב בעזרו	5 Happy is he who has the God of Jacob for his help,
שברו על־יהוה אלהיו:	whose hope is in the LORD his God,
עשה שמים וארץ	6 maker of heaven and earth,
את־הים ואת־כל־אשר־בם	the sea and all that is in them;
השמר אמת לעולם:	who keeps faith forever;
עשה משפט לעשוקים	7 who secures justice for those who are wronged,
נתן לחם לרעבים	gives food to the hungry.
יהוה מתיר אסורים:	The LORD sets prisoners free;
יהוה פקח עורים	8 the LORD restores sight to the blind;
יהוה זקף כפופים	the LORD makes those who are bent stand straight;
יהוה אהב צדיקים:	the LORD loves the righteous;
יהוה שמר את־גרים	9 the LORD watches over the stranger;
יתום ואלמנה יעודד	He gives courage to the orphan and widow,
ודרך רשעים יעות:	but makes the path of the wicked tortuous.
ימלך יהוה לעולם	10 The LORD shall reign forever,
אלהיך ציון לדר ודר	your God, O Zion, for all generations.
הללו־יה:	Hallelujah.

IF MAN IS MODERATE AND CONTENTED
THEN EVEN AGE IS NO BURDEN
IF HE IS NOT
THEN EVEN YOUTH IS
FULL OF CARES

PLATO

Composition 2, "Rustic Capitals," from *Our Calligraphic Heritage,* New York, Geyer Studio, 1979.

abcdefghijklmnopqurstvwxyz &
ectsſt ₹ſ ABCDEFGHIJKLMNOP
QVRSTWXYZ &AF

A Variation · abcdefghijklmnopqurſ
tvwxyz ₹ſ &ctg2sſt

ſemiformal · abcdefghijklmnopqurstvwx
yzsſsſtct ₹ſ ABCDEFGHIJKLMN
OPQVRSTWXYZ

Chart 11, "Humanistic Scripts," from *Our Calligraphic Heritage,* New York, Geyer Studio, 1979.

96

Composition 3, "Early Uncials," from *Our Calligraphic Heritage,* New York, Geyer Studio, 1979.

Chart 7, "Irish Half Uncials," from *Our Calligraphic Heritage,* New York, Geyer Studio, 1979.

Chart 14, "Seventeenth Century Script," from *Our Calligraphic Heritage,* New York, Geyer Studio, 1979.

Composition 13, "Fraktur Derivations," from *Our Calligraphic Heritage,* New York, Geyer Studio, 1979.

OXMOOR
HOUSE
Jericho

THE SOUTH BEHELD

Final rendering (top) and pencil sketches for display titling for *Jericho: The South Beheld*, Birmingham, AL, Oxmoor House, 1974.

Double-page spread from *The Family Haggadah for Passover*, showing the ten plagues, New York, Shunammite Press, 1998.

🖎 Today we are again involved in the re-examination of the values that calligraphy may have for us, for our society now and for the future. To a small extent, it is still an essential craft in that it fills some of the needs that seem to exist in our society. It is certainly also one of the sources and stimuli on which the graphic designer often falls back.

🖎 However if properly understood it can give a great deal of satisfaction to those who use it in the unique way in which self-expression can be fused with skill.

🖎 Writing, from the beginning, set out to convert speech into the visual. The quality of the visual in relation to time and place has been a challenge and will continue to challenge future calligraphers.

Chart 10, "From the writing of North Africa."

אבגדהוזח
טיכלמנסע
פצקרשת
סןוףץ

הלילי, נמרי, לו עיניה זולקות,
בחשך בחשך שמיו בורקות,
צפרן חזה-לו כתער,
נומה, ילדי, ביער!

Chart 28, "Oblique type."

משפע מכתבה פרסית

אבגדהוזחטיכל
מנסעפצקרשת
דףסשןוףףץ

אבגדהוזחטיכלמנס
עפצקרשת דסןוףץ

Chart 9, "From the writing of Persia."

Chart 13, "From the Sephardic tradition."

From *The Hebrew Letter: Calligraphic Variations*, Northvale, NJ, Jason Aronson, 1990.

ARCHITECTURAL
and three-dimensional design

❧ *Some of the smaller pieces allow me to do things that I couldn't possibly do in the larger works. To use strong decorative elements in a piece as large as* No Man Is An Island *would be impossible because the decorative elements would overwhelm the piece. But here, in one wall, in these few feet, I am in command of the situation — I can do anything I want within this limited area without being concerned about ruining the proportion. In that sense the smaller works are a far more personal statement as far as the actual lettering is concerned. And in that sense I am as pleased with the small pieces as I am with the large.*

Four of ten windows for Temple Beth El, Providence, RI, 1953. Designs on clear, rippled glass.

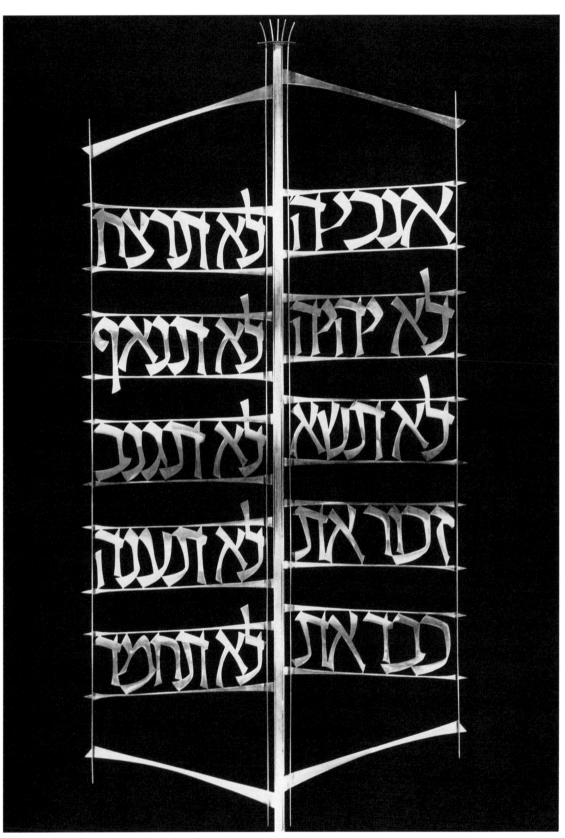

The "Ten Commandments." For the Daughters of Israel, Pleasant Valley Home, West Orange, NJ, 1961 or 1962. Metal.

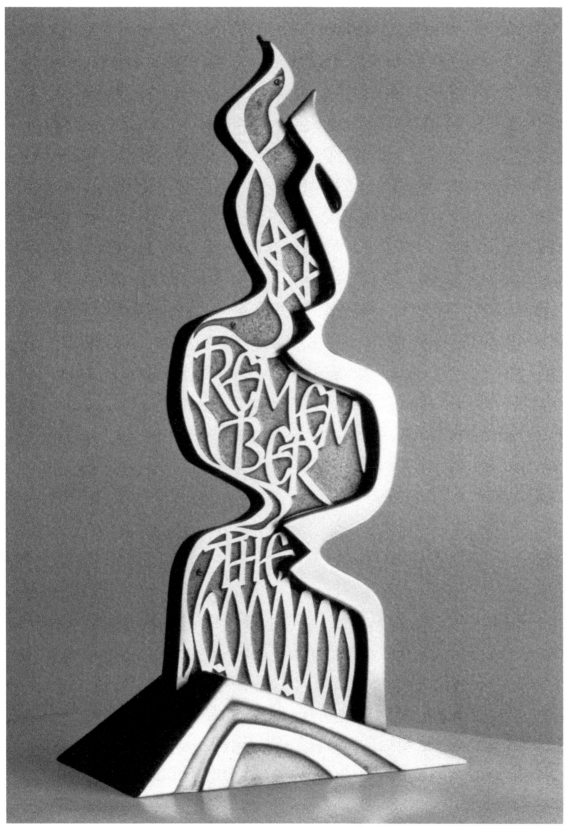

Sculpture [n.d.]. Bronze. The Hebrew letters for the word meaning "remember" frame the English text. This design can be read from both front and back.

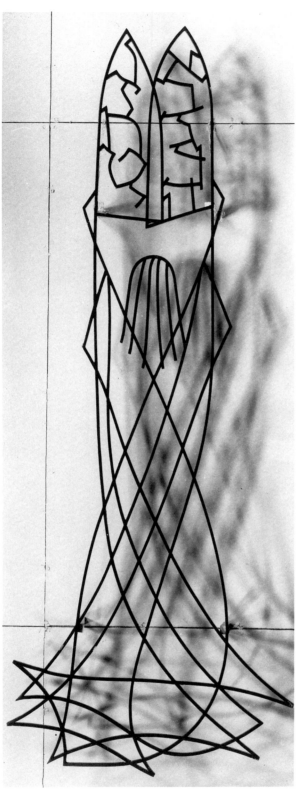

Wrought-iron figure of Moses for Beth Israel Cemetery, Woodbridge, NJ, 1956.

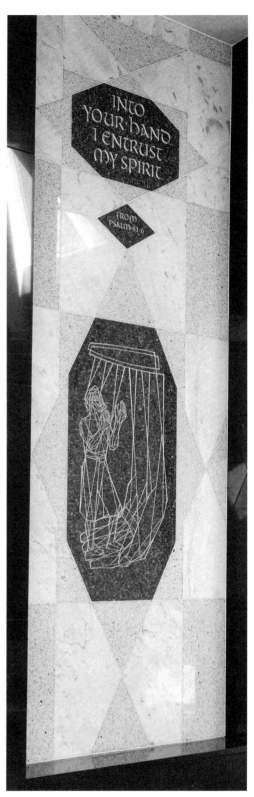

Stone mural in chapel area of mausoleum complex at Pinelawn Memorial Park, Farmingdale, NY, 1991. (Jerry L. Thompson, photography)

Artist's rendering of bronze doors for a private mausoleum at Beth Israel Cemetery, Woodbridge, NJ, 1967.

Architectural feature in the Garden of Hope at Pinelawn Memorial Park, Farmingdale, NY, 1979.
(Jerry L. Thompson, photography)

I think of No Man is an Island *as one of the great human statements. I felt compelled to render this text in a form that would not draw attention to its composition but rather to its content. I visualized a design of lines of equal length, filled with roman minuscules, the very forms the present-day reader is most familiar with.*

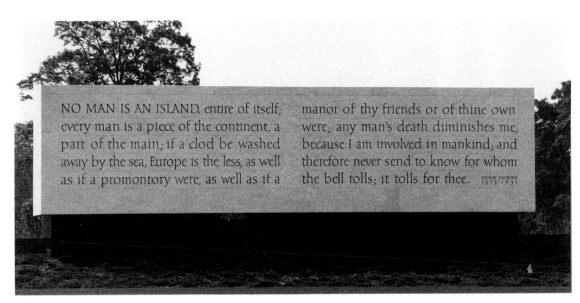

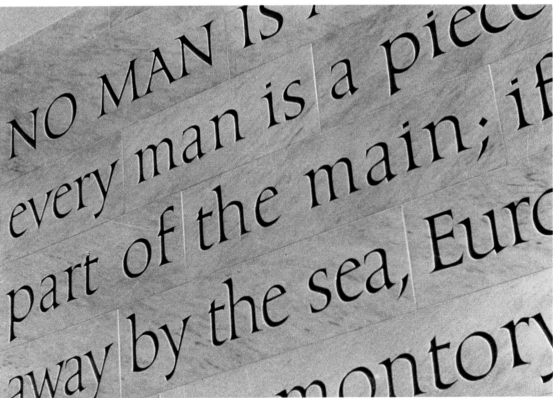

Detail of the inscription on *No Man Is An Island* mausoleum at Pinelawn Memorial Park, Farmingdale, NY, 1965–67. The x-height of the lowercase letters is approximately 7 inches.

Architectural feature in the Garden of Hymns at Pinelawn Memorial Park, Farmingdale, NY, 1966.

I think it is important to understand that the sculptural works you see at Pinelawn are industrial sculptures. They are defined by precise drawings that are measurable. They are executed by machines and in different locations, for example, in Italy, in New England or North Carolina. It would be impossible for me personally to explain all elements of the design to all of the craftsmen involved. With regard to the calligraphy, this often means that there is a certain degree of simplification that is necessary. If you want somebody to execute your drawing in stone, then the drawing should be free from the small idiosyncrasies that may hinder the stonecutting process. For example, to ask another hand to follow the flow from a large to a too-small curve is difficult. And so, when you work in stone, simplicity is both a virtue and, in many cases, a necessity.

Architectural feature in the Garden of Normandie at Pinelawn Memorial Park, Farmingdale, NY, 1978. (Jerry L. Thompson, photography)

Architectural feature in the Garden of Normandie at Pinelawn Memorial Park, Farmingdale, NY, 1978.

❧ There is no back. There is, of course, the main west view, but the east view is a focal point in its own right, enhanced by an inscription incised in dark granite. As in most of the pieces at Pinelawn, this feature can be approached, and viewed satisfactorily, from many directions and angles.

PAX ✦ PEACE

THIS STATUE, the bearer of peace
once adorned the interior of the great French liner
NORMANDIE. She had been the symbol of achievement in
French culture, art, engineering and industry. As a messenger of goodwill and
brotherhood she had called at ports around the world to be hailed and admired.
HER TRAGIC END came suddenly when at her pier in the Hudson River on
February the 9th, 1942 she was destroyed by fire. The statue survived the
disaster and found a new home in this park where she will be
an inspiring reminder of the ideals which the Normandie
embodied and stood for. To her memory
this garden is dedicated.

Design for metal plaque, Garden of Normandie, Pinelawn Memorial Park, Farmingdale, NY, 1978.

Fountain in chapel area of mausoleum complex at Pinelawn Memorial Park, Farmingdale, NY, 1986.
(Jerry L. Thompson, photography)

Fountain centerpiece of the Garden of Peace at Pinelawn Memorial Park, Farmingdale, NY, 1973.

From the outset, I knew that the design would have to use strong visual characteristics, because very often in windy or cold weather the water would be turned off... And so the elaborate shape of the fountain is purposeful, because it gives the fountain significance even when no water plays.

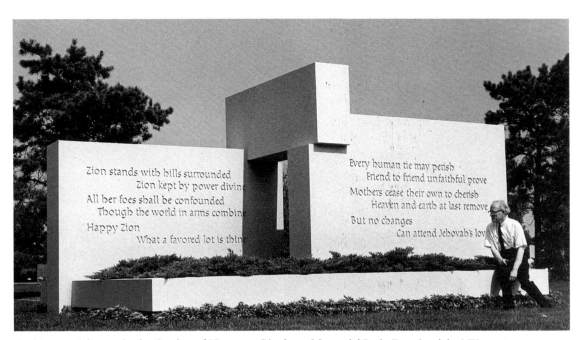

Zion stands with hills surrounded
Zion kept by power divine
All her foes shall be confounded
Though the world in arms combine
Happy Zion
What a favored lot is thine

Every human tie may perish
Friend to friend unfaithful prove
Mothers cease their own to cherish
Heaven and earth at last remove
But no changes
Can attend Jehovah's love

Architectural feature in the Garden of Hymns at Pinelawn Memorial Park, Farmingdale, NY, 1966.

Decorative wall in the Heritage Gardens at Pinelawn Memorial Park, Farmingdale, NY, 1969. (Jerry L. Thompson, photography)

Colonnade between sections of the mausoleum complex at Pinelawn Memorial Park, Farmingdale, NY, [n.d.]. (Jerry Thompson, photography)

Base for column feature in the Garden of Faith, Pinelawn Memorial Park, Farmingdale, NY, 1973. (Jerry L. Thompson, photography)

Interior of atrium at Pinelawn Memorial Park, Farmingdale, NY, 1983. The design includes wall ornaments, railing, skylights, and ceiling pattern. (Jerry L. Thompson, photography)

Decorative wall on the outside of mausoleum complex at Pinelawn Memorial Park, Farmingdale, NY, [n.d.]. (Jerry L. Thompson, photography)

❧ *On the opposite side of the same building are three panels of emerald green granite rendered with characters that have brought the rhythm of Irish half uncials into the 20th century. These characters are not copies of Irish half uncials. They are a very personal rendering using Irish form principals as motifs.*

118

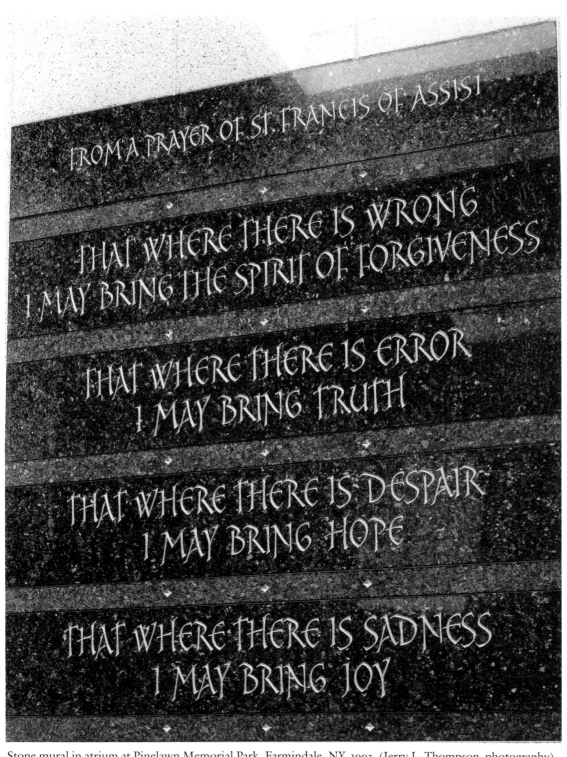

FROM A PRAYER OF ST. FRANCIS OF ASSISI

THAT WHERE THERE IS WRONG
I MAY BRING THE SPIRIT OF FORGIVENESS

THAT WHERE THERE IS ERROR
I MAY BRING TRUTH

THAT WHERE THERE IS DESPAIR
I MAY BRING HOPE

THAT WHERE THERE IS SADNESS
I MAY BRING JOY

Stone mural in atrium at Pinelawn Memorial Park, Farmindale, NY, 1993. (Jerry L. Thompson, photography)

Yahrzeit candle holder, 1957. Bronze.
"O merciful God."

Wall ornament, [n.d.]. Bronze.
"Listen Israel, the Lord is our God, the Lord is One."

Sanctuary of the Brotherhood Synagogue, New York, renovated 1994. The words "Holy, Holy, Holy" in Hebrew and English appear on the topmost panel with the Hebrew letter *shin*, symbol for the name of God filling the space underneath. The long frieze across the canopy carries the blessing from Numbers 6:24–26. The English translation is inscribed above the ark doors. The Ten Commandments symbolize the Torah scrolls within. Emblems for the twelve tribes of Israel flank the doors. (Jerry L. Thompson, photography)

The Holy Ark at the Brotherhood Synagogue, New York, 1994. Wood marquetry.
(Jerry L. Thompson, photography)

Design for Seder plate, with center inscription reading, "The Bread of Affliction," surrounded by the names of the six ceremonial foods.

Elijah cup, reading, "Elijah the prophet." Glass with silver base, [n.d.].

Sites with Ismar David's architectural work

A partial listing of locations in the United States

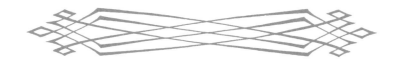

BETH EL SYNAGOGUE

Baltimore, Maryland
Decorative element, signage, ca. 1981–82.

**BETH ISRAEL CEMETERY
WOODBRIDGE MEMORIAL GARDENS**

Woodbridge, New Jersey
Feature design, mausoleum design, decorative
elements, overall layout, 1953–78.

BETH SHALOM CONGREGATION

Elkins Park, Pennsylvania
Hebrew word, *kadosh*, above the Ark, 1959.

BROTHERHOOD SYNAGOGUE

New York, New York
Ark, decorative elements, ramp to *bimah*, 1994.

**COMMUNITY CHURCH OF
NEW YORK**

New York, New York
Dr. and Mrs. John Haynes Holmes memorial
tablet, 1965–66.

**DAUGHTERS OF ISRAEL
PLEASANT VALLEY HOME**

West Orange, New Jersey
Decorative rendering of Ten Commandments,
ca. 1961.

**FOREST LAWN CEMETERY
& GARDEN MAUSOLEUMS**

Buffalo, New York
Mausoleum design, 1984–85.

KING DAVID CEMETERY

Putnam Valley, New York
Overall layout, decorative elements, 1964–71.

PARK AVENUE SYNAGOGUE

New York, New York
Inscriptions, signage, 1955.

PINELAWN MEMORIAL PARK

Farmingdale, New York
Overall layout, mausoleum design, decorative
features and elements, 1965–69.

SHARON MEMORIAL PARK

Sharon, Massachusetts
Plaster cast of the *Land of Israel* (1953) map in
bronze at Beth Israel cemetery.

**TEMPLE OF AARON
CONGREGATION**

St. Paul, Minnesota
Decorative elements, 1957–58.

TEMPLE EMANUEL

Beverly Hills, California
Decorative elements, 1955.

TEMPLE BETH EL

Providence, Rhode Island
Decorative elements, 1953.

TEMPLE SHALOM OF WEST ESSEX

Cedar Grove, New Jersey
Decorative elements, 1959–64.

Illustrations for *Poems from the German*, compiled by Helen Plotz, New York, Crowell 1967.

Illustrations for *The Twenty-third Psalm: An Interpretation*, by C.L. Allen, Westwood, NJ, Fleming H. Revell, 1961.

Bibliography

Compiled using correspondence, financial records, graphics and books in the Ismar David Archive in the Cary Collection, the following list comprises all known books on which Ismar David worked. A few titles have undoubtedly eluded the net and one or two may be here that should be swimming in other waters.

❧ *The following books were published in Israel (Palestine, before 1948) & include dust jacket or cover designs by Ismar David. The Hebrew citations are followed by translations:*

אדמס, ג׳. ט. האפוס של אמריקה.

Adams, James Truslow. *Epic of America.* Jerusalem: Mosad Bialik, [1947 or 1948]. 416 p., 24 cm. *Dust jacket design.*

בודנהיימר, שמעון. החי בארצות המקרא.

Bodenheimer, Friedrich Simon. *Animal Life in Biblical Lands.* 2 vols. Jerusalem: Mosad Bialik, [1949–56]. 24 cm. *Dust jacket design.*

גרנות, אברהם. בשדות הבנין.

Granott, Abraham. *In the Fields of the Structure.* Jerusalem: Mosad Bialik, [1951]. 270 p., 24 cm. *Dust jacket design.*

Lask, I.M., ed. and tr. *Palestine Stories.* Jerusalem: Tarshish Books, 1942. 223 p., 18 cm. *Paperback cover design.*

משנת הזוהר. נערך ומתורגם ע״י פ. לחובר וישעיה תשבי.

Mishnat ha-Zohar. Arranged and translated by Y. F. Lachower and I. Tishby. 2 vols. Jerusalem: Mosad Bialik, [1949–61]. 25 cm. *Dust jacket design.*

Nahon, S. U., ed. *Theodore Herzl, the Father of the Jewish State.* Prepared for publication by the Information Department of the Zionist Organisation and the Jewish Agency, Jerusalem. Tel-Aviv: Newman, 1950. [45] p., 28 cm. *Typography.*

פינסקר, י. ל. אוטואמנסיפציה.

Pinsker, Leon. *Auto-emancipation.* Jerusalem: Department of Youth and Pioneers of the Zionist Federation, [1951]. 71 p., 19 cm. *Cover design.*

ל״ה אשר נפלו בהרי חברון.

Thirty-five people who died in the Hebron Mountains when they rushed to help Gush Etzion on the 5th day of Shevat, 1948. Jerusalem: Department of Youth and Pioneers of the Zionist Federation, [1949 or 1950]. 262 p., 23 cm. *Dust jacket design.*

טורטשינר, נ. ה. ה. הלשון והספר.

Tur-Sinai, N.H. (Naphtali Herz). *The Language and the Book.* 3 vols. Jerusalem: Mosad Bialik, [1948–55]. 25 cm. *Dust jacket design.*

טברסקי, יוחנן. הבתולה מלודמיר.

Twersky, Yohanan. *The Virgin from Ludmir.* Jerusalem: Mosad Bialik, [1949]. 253 p., 19 cm. *Dust jacket design.*

The following books were produced in the United States and include designs by Ismar David as noted:

Abrams, Margaret. *Awakened: A Novel.* Philadelphia: Jewish Publication Society of America, 1954. 344 p., 22 cm. *Dust jacket design.*

Adler, Selig, and Thomas E. Connolly. *From Ararat to Suburbia: The History of the Jewish Community of Buffalo.* The Jacob R. Schiff Library of Jewish Contributions to American Democracy, no. 12. Philadelphia: Jewish Publication Society of America, 1960. 498 p., 24 cm. *Dust jacket design.*

Agar, Herbert. *The Saving Remnant: An Account of Jewish Survival.* New York: Viking Press, 1960. 269 p., 22 cm. *Dust jacket design.*

Agee, Jon. *The Incredible Painting of Felix Clousseau.* New York: Farrar, Straus and Giroux, 1988. 32 p., 26 cm. *Dust jacket and title page lettering.*

Albright, William Foxwell. *The Biblical Period from Abraham to Ezra.* Harper Torchbooks, TB 102. New York: Harper & Row, 1963. viii, 120 p., 20 cm. *Paperback cover design.*

Alexander, Franz, and Sheldon T. Selesnick. *The History of Psychiatry: An Evaluation of Psychiatric Thought and Practice from Prehistoric Times to the Present.* New York: Harper & Row, [1966]. xvi, 471 p., 25 cm. *Dust jacket design.*

Allen, Charles Livingstone. *All Things Are Possible Through Prayer.* [Westwood, NJ]: Fleming H. Revell, [1958]. 127 p., 21 cm. *Dust jacket design.*

——. *The Beatitudes: An Interpretation.* Illustrated by Ismar David. Westwood, NJ: Fleming H. Revell, [1967]. 61 p., 20 cm. *Dust jacket design; illustrations.*

——. *Healing Words.* Westwood, NJ: Fleming H. Revell, [1961]. 159 p., 21 cm. *Dust jacket design.*

——. *The Life of Christ.* Illustrated by Ismar David. Westwood, NJ: Fleming H. Revell, 1962. 157 p., 21 cm. *Dust jacket design; illustrations; binding illustrations.*

——. *The Lord's Prayer: An Interpretation.* Illustrated by Ismar David. [Westwood, NJ]: Fleming H. Revell, [1963]. 64 p., 20 cm. *Dust jacket design; illustrations.*

——. *Prayer Changes Things.* Westwood, NJ: Fleming H. Revell, [1964]. 128 p., 21 cm. *Dust jacket design.*

——. *The Sermon on the Mount.* Westwood, NJ: Fleming H. Revell, [1966]. 187 p., 21 cm. *Dust jacket design.*

——. *The Ten Commandments: An Interpretation.* Illustrated by Ismar David. [Westwood, NJ]: Fleming H. Revell, [1965]. 64 p., 21 cm. *Dust jacket design; illustrations and lettering.*

—— . *The Twenty-Third Psalm: An Interpretation*. Illustrated by Ismar David. [Westwood, NJ]: Fleming H. Revell, [1961]. 62 p., 20 cm. *Dust jacket design; illustrations.*

American Association of School Administrators. Commission on Religion in the Public Schools. *Religion in the Public Schools: A Report*. Harper ChapelBooks, cb13. New York: Harper & Row, 1965. x, 68 p., 21 cm. *Paperback cover design.*

Applegarth, Margaret Tyson, ed. *Heirlooms*. New York: Harper & Row, [1967]. 319 p., 25 cm. *Dust jacket design.*

Apuleius. *The Golden Ass*. Translated by Jack Lindsay. 1st Midland Book ed. Bloomington: Indiana University Press, 1962. 254 p., 20 cm. *Dust jacket design; also issued as paperback edition.*

Art Treasures of the World. 34 vols. New York: Abrams, 1952–1957. *Slipcase design, and design for corrugated mailing box.*

Astrachan, Samuel. *An End to Dying: A Novel*. New York: Farrar, Straus and Cudahy, [1956]. 246 p., 22 cm. *Dust jacket design; also issued as paperback edition.*

Auden, W. H., and Chester Kallman. *The Magic Flute: An Opera in Two Acts*. New York: Random House, [1956]. xv, 108 p., 24 cm. *Dust jacket design.*

Augustine, Saint, Bishop of Hippo. *The Confessions of St. Augustine*. Translated by Edward B. Pusey. Introduction by Harold C. Gardiner. New York: Washington Square Press, [1960]. xiv, 301 p., 17 cm. *Paperback cover design.*

Austen, Jane. *Pride and Prejudice*. With an introduction by M. Edmund Speare, and an afterword by W. Somerset Maugham. Pocket Library, pl9. New York: Pocket Books, 1954. vii, 436 p., 17 cm. *Paperback cover design.*

Bacon, Margaret Hope. *Lamb's Warrior: The Life of Isaac T. Hopper*. New York: T.Y. Crowell, [1970]. xiii, 207 p., 21 cm. *Dust jacket design.*

Baer, Yitzhak. *A History of the Jews in Christian Spain*. Translated from the Hebrew by Louis Schoffman. 2 vols. Philadelphia: Jewish Publication Society of America, 1961–66. 22 cm. *Dust jacket design.*

Bamberger, Bernard Jacob. *The Story of Judaism*. Commission on Jewish Education of the Union of American Hebrew Congregations and Central Conference of American Rabbis, Union Adult Series. New York: Union of American Hebrew Congregations, [1957]. 477 p., 24 cm. *Dust jacket design.*

Barclay, William. *The Apostles' Creed for Everyman*. [1st American ed.] New York: Harper & Row, [1967]. 384 p., 21 cm. *Dust jacket design.*

—— . *In the Hands of God*. Selected by Rita F. Snowden. Harper ChapelBooks, cb38. New York: Harper & Row, [1967]. 157 p., 21 cm. *Paperback cover design.*

—— . *The Life of Jesus for Everyman*. Harper ChapelBooks, cb27f. New York: Harper & Row, [1966]. 96 p., 21 cm. *Paperback cover design.*

—— . *Prayers for the Christian Year*. Harper ChapelBooks, cb9. New York: Harper & Row, [1965]. 175 p., 21 cm. *Paperback cover design.*

Barker, William Pierson. *As Matthew Saw the Master*. Westwood, NJ: Fleming H. Revell, [1964]. 154 p., 21 cm. *Dust jacket design.*

—— . *Kings in Shirtsleeves: Men Who Ruled Israel*. [Westwood, NJ]: Fleming H. Revell, [1961]. 119 p., 21 cm. *Dust jacket design.*

——. *Personalities Around Jesus*. [Westwood, NJ]: Fleming H. Revell, [1963]. 156 p., 20 cm. *Dust jacket design*.

——. *Saints in Aprons and Overalls: Friends of Paul*. [Westwood, NJ]: Fleming H. Revell, [1959]. 128 p., 21 cm. *Dust jacket design*.

——. *Twelve Who Were Chosen: The Disciples of Jesus*. [Westwood, NJ]: Fleming H. Revell, [1958]. 127 p., 21 cm. *Dust jacket design*.

Bazin, Germain. *A History of Art from Prehistoric Times to the Present*. Translated by Francis Scarfe. Boston: Houghton Mifflin, 1959. x, 574 p., 25 cm. *Dust jacket design*.

Bazin, Hervé. *Constance: A Novel*. Translated from the French by Herma Briffault. New York: Crown Publishers, [1955]. 216 p., 22 cm. *Dust jacket design*.

Beauvoir, Simone de. *Memoirs of a Dutiful Daughter*. Translated by James Kirkup. Cleveland: World Publishing Co., [1959]. 382 p., 24 cm. *Dust jacket design*.

Beek, Martinus Adrianus. *Concise History of Israel: From Abraham to the Bar Cochba Rebellion*. Translated by Arnold J. Pomerans. New York: Harper & Row, [1963]. 224 p., 21 cm. *Dust jacket design*.

Beimfohr, Herman N. *Prayers for Young People, for Personal or Group Worship*. [Westwood, NJ]: Fleming H. Revell, [1960]. 128 p., 27 cm. *Dust jacket design*.

Bellah, Robert Neelly. *Beyond Belief; Essays on Religion in a Post-Traditional World*. New York: Harper & Row, [1970]. xi, 298 p., 22 cm. *Dust jacket design*.

Ben-Yehuda, Ehud, ed. *Pocket English-Hebrew, Hebrew-English Dictionary*. New York: Washington Square Press, [1961]. 306, 320 p., 17 cm. *Paperback cover design*.

Bertin, Célia. *The Last Innocence*. Translated from the French by Marjorie Deans. New York: McGraw-Hill, 1955. 305 p., 21 cm. *Dust jacket design*.

Bible. *The Book of Ecclesiastes*. King James Version (rev.). With an introduction by Kenneth Rexroth and illustrated by Edgar Miller. New York: Limited Editions Club, 1968. 53 p., 31 cm. *Leather binding design; Hebrew lettering and decorative element for title page*.

——. *The Book of Esther*. Introduction by H. L. Ginsberg. Philadelphia: Jewish Publication Society, 1969. 32 p., 19 cm. *Booklet design; cover design; illustration*.

——. *The Book of Jeremiah*. A new translation, with woodcuts by Nikos Stavroulakis. Introduction by Bernard J. Bamberger. Philadelphia: Jewish Publication Society of America, [1973]. xv, 93 p., 34 cm. *Book design; dust jacket design; numbers*.

——. *Book of Job: A Commentary*, by Solomon B. Freehof. Commission on Jewish Education of the Union of American Hebrew Congregations and the Central Conference of American Rabbis, Union Adult Series, New York: Union of American Hebrew Congregations, 1958. 261 p., 24 cm. *Binding design*.

——. *The Book of Jonah*. Drawings and design by Ismar David; with an introduction by Chaim Potok. Southbury, CT: Chiswick Book Shop, 1991. xii, 17 p., 31 cm. *Book and binding design; illustration*.

——. *Book of Kings 1: A Commentary*, by Leo L. Honor. Commission on Jewish Education of the Union of American Hebrew Congregations and the Central Conference of American Rabbis, Union Adult Series, New York: Union of American Hebrew Congregations, 1955. xiii, 367 p., 24 cm. *Binding design.*

——. *Book of Proverbs: A Commentary*, by W. Gunther Plaut. Commission on Jewish Education of the Union of American Hebrew Congregations and the Central Conference of American Rabbis, Union Adult Series, New York: Union of American Hebrew Congregations, 1961. xi, 339 p., 24 cm. *Binding design.*

——. *The Book of Psalms: A New Translation According to the Traditional Hebrew Text*. Philadelphia: Jewish Publication Society of America, [1972]. vi, 151 p., 24 cm. *Book and dust jacket design; lettering.*

——. *Daniel 3 from the Holy Bible, King James Version*. Typography by Joseph Trautwein with decorations by Ismar David. [Cleveland: World Publishing Co., 1954]. [16] p., 25 cm. Edition limited to 1,250 numbered copies. *Illustration; design for slipcase; lettering.*

——. *The Five Megilloth and Jonah: A New Translation*. Introductions by H. L. Ginsberg; with drawings by Ismar David. Philadelphia: Jewish Publication Society of America, 1969, and 2nd rev. ed., 1974. xi, 121 p., 24 cm. *Book design; dust jacket design; text illustrations; chapter titles; numbers.*

——. *The Holy Scriptures According to the Masoretic Text*. 2 vols. Philadelphia: Jewish Publication Society of America, 1955. xv, 2,264 p., 22 cm. *Lettering for title page and binding.*

——. *The Holy Scriptures According to the Masoretic Text: A New Translation with the Aid of Previous Versions and with the Constant Consultation of Jewish Authorities*. Philadelphia: Jewish Publication Society of America, 1958. xv, 1,136 p., 19 cm. *Dust jacket design.*

——. *The Holy Scriptures According to the Masoretic Text: A New Translation with the Aid of Previous Versions and with the Constant Consultation of Jewish Authorities*. Philadelphia: Jewish Publication Society of America, [1967]. 1,136 p., 19 cm. *Dust jacket design; binding design.*

——. *Pardes Torah: A Jewish Commentary on the Torah. Genesis*. Commentary by W. Gunther Plaut. New York: The Union of American Hebrew Congregations, 1973. 28 p., 25 cm. *Hebrew titling.*

——. *The Psalms. A New English Translation Prepared by the Jewish Publication Society of America*. Issued on the occasion of the one-hundredth anniversary of the Union of American Hebrew Congregations, with drawings by Ismar David. New York: Union of American Hebrew Congregations, 1973. x, 178 p., 34 cm. *Book design; illustrations; binding design; calligraphy; endpapers.*

——. *The Prophets. A New Translation of the Holy Scriptures According to the Masoretic Text: Second Section.* Philadelphia: Jewish Publication Society of America, 1978. xviii, 898 p., 22 cm. *Dust jacket design; title and half-title designs; binding design; Hebrew lettering.*

——. *A Shortened Arrangement of the Holy Bible.* Revised Standard Version edited by Robert O. Ballou. Philadelphia: Published by A.J. Holman Co., for Lippincott, 1964. xxxii, 773 p., 22 cm. *Dust jacket design; title and half-title designs; binding design; Hebrew lettering.*

——. *The Torah: The Five Books of Moses.* Philadelphia: Jewish Publication Society of America, 1962. 393 p., 22 cm. *Dust jacket design; title and half-title designs; binding design; Hebrew lettering.*

——. *The Torah: A Modern Commentary.* Commentaries by W. Gunther Plaut and Bernard J. Bamberger. Essays on Ancient Near Eastern Literature by William W. Hallo. New York: The Union of American Hebrew Congregations, 1981. 1,787 p., 26 cm. *Hebrew titling.*

——. *The Writings: A New Translation of the Holy Scriptures According to the Masoretic Text: Third Section.* Philadelphia: Jewish Publication Society of America, 1982. vii, 624 p., 22 cm. *Dust jacket design; title and half-title designs; binding design; Hebrew lettering.*

The Biblical Expositor: The Living Theme of the Great Book, with General and Introductory Essays and Exposition for Each Book of the Bible. Carl F. H. Henry, consulting editor. 3 vols. Philadelphia: A. J. Holman, [1960]. 24 cm. *Dust jacket design.*

Binstock, Louis. *The Road to Successful Living.* New York: Simon and Schuster, 1958. 307 p., 22 cm. *Dust jacket design.*

Blankfort, Michael. *The Strong Hand.* Boston: Little, Brown, [1956]. 318 p., 22 cm. *Dust jacket design.*

Bodley, Ronald Victor Courtenay. *In Search of Serenity.* Boston: Little, Brown, [1955]. 176 p., 21 cm. *Dust jacket design.*

Bolton, Sarah Knowles. *Famous Men of Science.* Revised by Barbara Lovett Cline. 4th ed. New York: T.Y. Crowell, [1961]. 326 p., 21 cm. *Dust jacket design.*

Bonnell, John Sutherland, et al. *He Speaks From the Cross: The Seven Last Words.* [Westwood, NJ]: Fleming H. Revell, [1963]. 126 p., 21 cm. *Dust jacket design.*

Bonnell, John Sutherland. *No Escape from Life.* Harper ChapelBooks, cb14j. New York: Harper & Row, [1965]. 215 p., 22 cm. *Paperback cover design.*

Bowers, Claude Gernade. *Chile Through Embassy Windows, 1939–1953.* New York: Simon and Schuster, 1958. ix, 375 p., 24 cm. *Dust jacket design.*

Bristol, Lee Hastings. *Seed for a Song.* Boston: Little, Brown, [1958]. 244 p., 21 cm. *Dust jacket design.*

Bro, Margueritte Harmon. *More Than We Are.* Rev. and enl. ed. Harper ChapelBooks, cb7. New York: Harper & Row, [1965]. 177 p., 21 cm. *Paperback cover design.*

Brodkey, Harold. *First Love and Other Sorrows.* New York: Dial Press, [1957]. 223 p., 20 cm. *Dust jacket design.*

Brokhoff, John R. *This is Life.* Westwood, NJ: Fleming H. Revell, [1959]. 126 p., 21 cm. *Dust jacket design.*

Brontë, Charlotte. *Jane Eyre.* 3rd ed. New York: Washington Square Press, 1960. viii, 517 p., 17 cm. *Paperback cover design.*

Bruce, Claire. *A Spirit Drawing, by Claire Bruce, Rendered Posthumously*. New York: Privately Printed, 1960. [4] l, 38 cm. 100 copies of this book printed by James Hendrickson at the press of William E. Rudges's Sons, New York. *Lettering for binding.*

Buck, Pearl S. *Fourteen Stories*. Giant Cardinal edition. New York: Pocket Books, 1963. 229 p., 16 cm. *Paperback cover design.*

Buckmaster, Henrietta. *And Walk in Love: A Novel Based on the Life of the Apostle Paul*. New York: Random House, [1956]. 404 p., 22 cm. *Dust jacket design.*

Buckler, William Earl. *Novels in the Making*. Literature in the Making series. Boston: Houghton Mifflin, 1961. 266 p., 21 cm. *Paperback cover design.*

Bunch, Josephine, and Christopher Bunch. *Prayers for the Family*. [Westwood, NJ]: Fleming H. Revell, [1961]. 62 p., 17 cm. *Dust jacket design.*

Burnham, George. *To The Far Corners: With Billy Graham in Asia, Including Excerpts from Billy Graham's Diary*. [Westwood, NJ]: Fleming H. Revell, [1956]. 160 p., 22 cm. *Dust jacket design.*

Butler, G. Paul, ed. *Best Sermons: 1955 Edition*. New York: McGraw-Hill, 1955. xvi, 341 p., 22 cm. *Dust jacket design.*

Campenhausen, Hans, Freiherr von. *Men Who Shaped the Western Church*. Translated by Manfred Hoffman. New York: Harper & Row, [1964]. vii, 328 p., 22 cm. *Dust jacket design.*

Capers, Gerald Mortimer. *Stephen A. Douglas, Defender of the Union*. Edited by Oscar Handlin. Boston: Little, Brown, [1959]. 239 p., 21 cm. *Dust jacket design.*

Capote, Truman. *Breakfast at Tiffany's: A Short Novel and Three Stories*. New York: Random House, [1958]. 179 p., 21 cm. *Dust jacket design.*

Carrighar, Sally. *Moonlight at Midday*. New York: Knopf, 1958. 392 p., 22 cm. *Dust jacket design.*

Cartwright, John K. *The Catholic Shrines of Europe*. With photos by Alfred Wagg. Foreword by Martin J. O'Connor. New York: McGraw-Hill, [1955]. 212 p., 26 cm. *Dust jacket design.*

Chotzinoff, Samuel. *A Lost Paradise: Early Reminiscences*. New York: Knopf, 1955. 373 p., 22 cm. *Dust jacket design.*

Clad, Noel. *Love and Money*. New York: Random House, [1959]. 525 p., 22 cm. *Dust jacket design.*

Clark, Walter Van Tilburg. *The Ox-Bow Incident*. Modern Library paperbacks, p31. New York: Random House, [1957]. 309 p., 19 cm. *Paperback cover design.*

Coffman, James Burton. *The Ten Commandments, Yesterday and Today*. [Westwood, NJ]: Fleming H. Revell, [1961]. 128 p., 21 cm. *Dust jacket design.*

Cohen, Hermann. *Religion of Reason: Out of the Sources of Judaism*. Translated and with an introduction by Simon Kaplan. New York: F. Ungar, [1972]. xliii, 489 p., 25 cm. *Dust jacket design.*

Coleridge, Samuel Taylor. *Coleridge's Writings on Shakespeare: A Selection of the Essays, Notes and Lectures of Samuel Taylor Coleridge on the Poems and Plays of Shakespeare*. Newly edited and arranged by Terence Hawkes. Putnam Capricorn book, cap ii. New York: Capricorn Books, [1959]. 256 p., 19 cm. *Paperback cover design.*

Collyer, Bud. *Thou Shalt Not Fear*. Westwood, NJ: Fleming H. Revell, 1962. 64 p., 20 cm. *Dust jacket design.*

Comparative Education Society. *The Changing Soviet School: The Comparative Education Society Field Study in the USSR*. Edited by George Z.F. Bereday, et al. Boston: Houghton Miffin; Constable, 1960. 514 p., 23 cm. *Dust jacket design.*

Constantin, Prince of Bavaria. *After the Flood*. Translated from the German by Constantine Fitzgibbon. Philadelphia: Lippincott, 1955. 224 p., 21 cm. *Dust jacket design.*

Cooney, Barbara. *The American Speller: An Adaptation of Noah Webster's Blue-backed Speller*. Illustrated by Barbara Cooney. New York: T.Y. Crowell, [1960]. 77 p., 23 cm. *Lettering for dust jacket.*

Corcoran, Barbara. *The Sky is Falling*. New York: Atheneum, 1988. 185 p., 21 cm. *Book and jacket design; chapter titles; decorative initials.*

Cotterell, Geoffrey. *Errand at Shadow Creek*. Philadelphia: Lippincott, 1959. 255 p., 21 cm. *Dust jacket design.*

Clifford, James Lowry. *Young Sam Johnson*. New York: McGraw-Hill, [1955]. 377 p., 21 cm. *Dust jacket design.*

Dahl, Borghild. *I Wanted to See*. [New York]: Macmillan, 1967. 210 p., 21 cm. *Dust jacket design.*

David, Ismar. *The Hebrew Letter: Calligraphic Variations*. Northvale, NJ: J. Aronson Inc., 1990. 86 p., 32 charts, 23 cm. *Book and box design; charts; graphics.*

——. *Our Calligraphic Heritage: The Geyer Studio Writing Book: Text, Charts, and Compositions*. New York: Geyer Studio, Inc., 1979. 1 portfolio (37 p., [17] leaves, [68] p.), 24 cm. *Book and case design; charts; compositions.*

——. *Reflections: Six Drawings of Themes from the Holy Scriptures*. [Philadelphia]: Jewish Publication Society of America, [1969?]. 1 portfolio ([2] leaves, [6] leaves of plates), 32 cm. *Portfolio design.*

Delaney, John J., ed. *A Woman Clothed with the Sun: Eight Great Appearances of Our Lady in Modern Times*. Garden City, NY: Image Books, [1961]. 274 p., 18 cm. *Paperback cover design.*

DeVegh, Elizabeth Baynes. *The Eye of the Beholder, and Other Stories*. New York: Random House, [1957]. 182 p., 21 cm. *Dust jacket design.*

——. *A Knot of Roots*. New York: Random House, [1958]. 314 p., 21 cm. *Dust jacket design.*

DeWohl, Louis. *The Quiet Light*. Garden City, NY: Image Books, 1958. 319 p., 18 cm. *Paperback cover design.*

Dickinson, Emily. *Poems of Emily Dickinson*. Selected by Helen Plotz, with drawings by Robert Kipniss. New York: T.Y. Crowell, 1964. xvii, 157 p., 21 cm. *Dust jacket design.*

Donaldson, W. Albert. *You Can Love Again*. Anderson, IN: Warner Press, 1959. 139 p., 20 cm. *Dust jacket design.*

Dostoyevsky, Fyodor. *Great Short Works of Fyodor Dostoevsky*. Introduction by Ronald Hingley. Harper Perennial Classic, p3081. New York: Harper & Row, 1968. xiii, 741 p., 18 cm. *Paperback cover lettering.*

Doulis, Thomas. *The Quarries of Sicily*. New York: Crown Publishers, [1969]. 176 p., 22 cm. *Dust jacket design.*

Dreznits, Shelomoh. *Tales in Praise of the ARI*. Translated from the Hebrew by Aaron Klein and Jenny Machlowitz Klein. Drawings by Moshe Raviv. Philadelphia: Jewish Publication Society of America, 1970. 62 p., 34 cm. *Book design; dust jacket design; decorative initials.*

Eastman, Max. *Great Companions: Critical Memoirs of Some Famous Friends*. New York: Farrar, Straus and Cudahy, 1959. 312 p., [12] leaves of plates, 22 cm. *Dust jacket design.*

TAISIE or IYONL

Ehrlich, Ernst Ludwig. *A Concise History of Israel from the Earliest Times to the Destruction of the Temple in A. D. 70*. Translated by James Barr. Harper Torchbooks, T B 128; The Cloister Library. New York: Harper & Row, [1965]. 153 p., 21 cm. *Paperback cover design.*

Eisenstein, Judith Kaplan. *Heritage of Music: The Music of the Jewish People*. New York: Union of American Hebrew Congregations, [1972]. xix, 339 p., 29 cm. *Dust jacket design.*

Eisenberg, Azriel Louis, comp. *Eyewitnesses to Jewish History; from 586 B.C.E. to 1967*. Edited by Azriel Eisenberg, Hannah Grad Goodman and Alvin Kass. New York: Union of American Hebrew Congregations, [1973]. xiv, 457 p., 24 cm. *Cover design.*

Eisenberg, Azriel, and Hannah Grad Goodman, ed. *Eyewitnesses to American Jewish History: A History of American Jewry*. 4 vols. New York: Union of American Hebrew Congregations, 1976–82. 24 cm. *Paperback cover design.*

Eldad, Israel, and Moshe Aumann, ed. *Chronicles; News of the Past*. 3 vols. Jerusalem: Reubeni Foundation, [1954–]. 34 cm. *Masthead design.*

Elliot, Elisabeth. *Through Gates of Splendor*. Harper ChapelBooks, C B 101. New York: Harper, 1965. 258 p., 21 cm. *Paperback cover design.*

Emerson, Ralph Waldo. *The Portable Emerson*. Selected and arranged with an introduction and notes by Mark Van Doren. Viking Portable Library, P 25. [New York]: Viking Press, 1956. 664 p., 18 cm. *Paperback cover design.*

Engler, Richard E. *The Challenge of Diversity*. New York: Harper & Row, [1964]. xiv, 338 p., 22 cm. *Dust jacket design.*

Evans, Louis Hadley. *Life's Hidden Power: The Gift of the Spirit*. [Westwood, NJ]: Fleming H. Revell, [1958]. 154 p., 21 cm. *Dust jacket design.*

Evans, Louis Hadley. *Your Marriage – Duel or Duet?* [Westwood, NJ]: Fleming H. Revell, [1962]. 128 p., 21 cm. *Dust jacket design.*

The Family Haggadah for Passover. Drawings and design by Ismar David; with Hebrew calligraphy by Helen Brandshaft. New York: Shunammite Press, 1998. 96 p., 23 cm. *Book design; illustration; lettering.*

Fast, Howard. *Moses, Prince of Egypt*. New York: Crown Publishers, [1958]. 303 p., 22 cm. *Dust jacket design.*

Faulkner, William. *Sartoris*. New York: Random House, [1956]. 379 p., 21 cm. *Dust jacket design.*

Faure, Raoul Cohen. *Summer of Stones, A Novel*. New York: Crown Publishers, [1964]. 288 p., 22 cm. *Dust jacket design.*

Faverty, Frederic Everett. *Your Literary Heritage*. Philadelphia: Lippincott, [1959]. 254 p., 21 cm. *Dust jacket design.*

Ferguson, Wallace Klippert, and Geoffrey Bruun. *A Survey of European Civilization*. 3rd ed. 2 vols. Boston: Houghton Mifflin, 1958. 25 cm. *Binding design; illustration.*

Fey, Harold Edward. *The Lord's Supper: Seven Meanings: Memorial, Thanksgiving, Covenant, Affirmation, Spiritual Strength, Atonement, Immortality*. Harper ChapelBooks, TB5. New York: Harper & Row, 1965. 117 p., 21 cm. *Paperback cover design.*

Fields, Harvey J. *With All Your Heart*. New York: Union of American Hebrew Congregations, 1976, 1979. xvi, 171 p., 29 cm. *Paperback cover design of 1976 edition; changes and additional lettering for title page, 1979 edition.*

Filmus, Tully. *Tully Filmus: Selected Drawings*. With an essay by Isaac Bashevis Singer. Introduction by George Albert Perret. Philadelphia: Jewish Publication Society of America, 1971. xx, 76 p., 34 cm. *Book design, dust jacket design; chapter titles; paperback cover design.*

Finkelstein, Louis, ed. *The Jews: Their History, Culture, and Religion*. 3rd ed. 2 vols. New York: Harper & Row, [1960]. 24 cm. *Dust jacket design.*

Finley, Moses I. *The World of Odysseus*. New York: Viking Press, 1954. 179 p., 22 cm. *Dust jacket design.*

Flaubert, Gustave. *Madame Bovary*. A New Translation by Francis Steegmuller. New York: Random House, [1957]. xv, 396 p., 21 cm. *Dust jacket design.*

Fleming, Alice Mulcahey. *The Senator from Maine: Margaret Chase Smith*. Women of America series. New York: Crowell, [1969]. 136 p., 22 cm. *Dust jacket design.*

Forsee, Aylesa. *Pablo Casals: Cellist for Freedom*. New York: T.Y. Crowell, [1965]. 229 p., 21 cm. *Dust jacket design.*

Fosdick, Harry Emerson. *The Living of These Days: An Autobiography*. Harper ChapelBooks, CB33. New York: Harper & Row, 1967. ix, 324 p., 21 cm. *Paperback cover design.*

——. *The Man from Nazareth as His Contemporaries Saw Him*. Harper ChapelBooks, CB8. New York: Harper & Row, [1965]. 277 p., 21 cm. *Paperback cover design.*

——. *On Being a Real Person*. Harper ChapelBooks, CB2. New York: Harper & Row, 1965. xiv, 295 p., 20 cm. *Paperback cover design.*

——. *The Secret of Victorious Living*. Harper ChapelBooks, CB19h. New York: Harper & Row, 1966. vi, 208 p., 21 cm. *Paperback cover design.*

Fox, Emmet. *Make Your Life Worth While*. Harper ChapelBooks, CB34. New York: Harper & Row, 1967. ix, 239 p., 21 cm. *Paperback cover design.*

Franklin, Denson N. *Faith for These Troubled Times*. [Westwood, NJ]: Fleming H. Revell, [1958]. 123 p., 21 cm. *Dust jacket design.*

Freedgood, Lillian. *Great Artists of America*. New York: T.Y. Crowell, [1963]. xvi, 253 p., 26 cm. *Dust jacket design.*

Freehof, Solomon Bennett. *A Treasury of Responsa*. Philadelphia: Jewish Publication Society of America, 1963. 313 p., 22 cm. *Dust jacket design.*

French, Edward L., and J. Clifford Scott. *Child in the Shadows: A Manual for Parents of Retarded Children*. Philadelphia: Lippincott, [1960]. 156 p., 21 cm. *Dust jacket design*.

Friedlander, Albert H. *The Path of Faithfulness; A Service of Prayer*. [New York: Union of American Hebrew Congregations], 1973. 21 p., 28 cm. *Illustrations from* The Psalms *(1973)*.

Fuller, Charles Edward. *Ruth: A Life of Love and Loyalty*. [Westwood, NJ]: Fleming H. Revell, [1959]. 123 p., 20 cm. *Dust jacket design*.

Funk, Robert Walter, ed. *The Bultmann School of Biblical Interpretation: New Directions? With an Essay Introducing Journal for Theology and the Church*. Harper Torchbooks, TB 251. New York: Harper and Row, 1965. 183 p., 21 cm. Issued as *Journal for Theology and the Church*, v. 1. *Paperback cover design*.

——. *Distinctive Protestant and Catholic Themes Reconsidered*. Harper Torchbooks, TB 253. New York: Harper & Row; Tübingen: J.C.B. Mohr (Paul Siebeck), 1967. 164 p., 21 cm. Issued as *Journal for Theology and the Church*, v. 3. *Paperback cover design*.

——. *God and Christ: Existence and Province*. Harper Torchbooks, TB 255. New York: Harper & Row; Tübingen: J.C.B. Mohr (Paul Siebeck), 1968. 154 p., 21 cm. Issued as *Journal for Theology and the Church*, v. 5. *Paperback cover design*.

——. *History and Hermeneutic*. Harper Torchbooks, TB 254. New York: Harper & Row; Tübingen: J.C.B. Mohr (Paul Siebeck), 1967. 162 p., 21 cm. Issued as *Journal for Theology and the Church*, v. 4. *Paperback cover design*.

——. *Translating Theology into the Modern Age; [Historical, Systematic and Pastoral Reflections on Theology and the Church in the Contemporary Situation*, by Rudolf Bultmann, et al.] Harper Torchbooks, TB 252. New York: Harper & Row; Tübingen: J.C.B. Mohr (Paul Siebeck), 1965. 179 p., 21 cm. Issued as *Journal for Theology and the Church*, v. 2. *Paperback cover design*.

Garth, David. *The Watch on the Bridge: A Novel*. New York: Putnam, [1959]. 320 p., 21 cm. *Dust jacket design*.

Gassner, John. *Theatre and Drama in the Making*. Literature in the Making series. 2 vols. Boston: Houghton Mifflin, 1964. 21 cm. *Paperback cover design*.

——. *Theatre and Drama in the Making*. "Augmented" hardcover ed. Boston: Houghton Mifflin, 1964. xvi, 1,071 p., 22 cm. *Lettering for binding and title page*.

Gay, Ruth. *Perspectives on the American Jewish Experience: A Syllabus*. New York: National Council of Jewish Women, 1976. vii, 26 p., 28 cm. *Paperback cover design*.

Gibson, W. Walker. *Poems in the Making*. Literature in the Making series. Boston: Houghton Mifflin, 1963. 224 p., 21 cm. *Paperback cover design*.

Ginzburg, Louis. *On Jewish Law and Lore*. Philadelphia: Jewish Publication Society of America, 1955. 262 p., 21 cm. *Dust jacket design*.

Gittelsohn, Roland Bertram. *Wings of the Morning*. Illustrated by Ismar David. Commission on Jewish Education of the Union of American Hebrew Congregations and Central Conference of American Rabbis, Union Graded Series. New York: Union of American Hebrew Congregations, [1969]. xii, 387 p., 25 cm. *Design and lettering for binding; illustrations; chapter titles*.

Golden, Harry. *Carl Sandburg*. Cleveland: World Publishing Co., [1961]. 287 p., 22 cm. *Dust jacket design*.

Goodrich, Robert Edward. *Reach for the Sky: Life at Its Highest*. [Westwood, NJ]: Fleming H. Revell, [1960]. 126 p., 21 cm. *Dust jacket design*.

Goyen, William. *The Faces of Blood Kindred: A Novella and Ten Stories*. [New York]: Random House, [1960]. 167 p., 21 cm. *Dust jacket design*.

Graham, Lorenz B. *I, Momolu*. Illustrated by John Biggers. New York: T. Y. Crowell, [1966]. 226 p., 21 cm. *Dust jacket design*.

Granat, Robert. *The Important Thing*. New York: Random House, [1961]. 343 p., 21 cm. *Dust jacket design*.

Grayzel, Solomon. *A History of the Jews, from the Babylonian Exile to the End of World War II*. Philadelphia: Jewish Publication Society of America, 1960. xxv, 843 p., 22 cm. *Dust jacket design*.

Gregg, Josiah. *Commerce of the Prairies*. Introduction by Archibald Hanna. Keystone Western Americana Series, KB 52–53. 2 vols. Philadelphia: Lippincott, [1962]. 21 cm. *Dust jacket design; also issued as paperback edition*.

Griffith, Arthur Leonard. *Encounters with Christ: The Personal Ministry of Jesus*. Harper ChapelBooks, CB 29. New York: Harper & Row, 1966. 158 p., 20 cm. *Paperback cover design*.

Griffith, Jeannette. *Dearest Kate: A Catholic Girl Meets the Problems of Manners and Morals*. Philadelphia: Lippincott, [1961]. 172 p., 21 cm. *Dust jacket design*.

Guitton, Jean. *Great Heresies and Church Councils*. Translated by F.D. Wieck. New York: Harper & Row, [1965]. 191 p., 22 cm. *Dust jacket design*.

Guthrie, A.B. *The Way West*. New York: Pocket Library, 1955. 435 p., 17 cm. *Paperback cover design*.

Guttmacher, Alan Frank. *Pregnancy and Birth: A Book for Expectant Parents*. New York: Viking Press, 1957. xvi, 335 p., 22 cm. *Dust jacket design*.

Guttmann, Alexander. *The Struggle Over Reform in Rabbinic Literature During the Last Century and a Half*. Foreword by Solomon B. Freehof. Jerusalem and New York: World Union for Progressive Judaism, 1977. xxvii, 382 p., 24 cm. *Dust jacket design*.

Hall, Arthur Dana. *The Golden Balance*. New York: Crown Publishers, [1955]. 280 p., 22 cm. *Dust jacket design*.

Hall, Ennen Reaves. *Gifts from the Bible*. Drawings by Ismar David. New York: Harper & Row, [1968]. 114 p., 27 cm. *Dust jacket design; illustrations*.

Hamilton, James Wallace. *Who Goes There? What and Where Is God?* [Westwood, NJ]: Fleming H. Revell, [1958]. 154 p., 22 cm. *Dust jacket design*.

Han, Suyin. *The Mountain Is Young*. New York: Putnam, [1958]. 511 p., 22 cm. *Dust jacket design*.

Handlin, Oscar. *Adventure in Freedom: Three Hundred Years of Jewish Life in America*. New York: McGraw-Hill, [1954]. 282 p., 21 cm. *Dust jacket design*.

Hansen, Marcus Lee. *The Immigrant in American History*. Harper Torchbooks, TB 1120. New York: Harper & Row, [1964]. 230 p., 21 cm. *Paperback cover design*.

Hardy, Thomas. *Great Short Works of Thomas Hardy*. Harper Perennial Classic, P 3076. New York: Harper & Row, [1967]. 387 p., 18 cm. *Paperback cover lettering*.

Harrison, R. K. *Archaeology of the Old Testament.* Harper ChapelBooks, CB24G. New York: Harper & Row, [1966]. 162 p., 20 cm. *Paperback cover design.*

Hausner, Gideon. *Justice in Jerusalem.* New York: Harper & Row, [1966]. xiii, 528 p., 25 cm. *Dust jacket design.*

Havner, Vance. *Truth for Each Day: Meditations for Every Day of the Year.* Westwood, NJ: Fleming H. Revell, 1960. 270 p., 17 cm. *Dust jacket design.*

Hawthorne, Nathaniel. *The House of the Seven Gables.* Pocket Library PL15. New York: Pocket Books, 1954. viii, 370 p., 17 cm. *Paperback cover design.*

Hazelton, Roger. *New Accents in Contemporary Theology.* Harper ChapelBooks, CB17. New York: Harper & Row, 1965. 144 p., 22 cm. *Paperback cover design.*

Head, Ann. *Fair with Rain: A Novel.* New York: McGraw-Hill, [1957]. 181 p., 21 cm. *Dust jacket design.*

Heller, James Gutheim. *Isaac M. Wise: His Life, Work, and Thought.* New York: Union of American Hebrew Congregations, [1965]. xxi, 819 p., 21 cm. *Dust jacket design.*

Hemingway, Ernest. *Green Hills of Africa.* Garden City, NY: Permabooks, [1954]. 199 p., 18 cm. *Paperback cover design.*

Henrichsen, Margaret. *Seven Steeples.* Illustrated by William Barss. Harper ChapelBooks, CB36. New York: Harper & Row, 1967. 238 p., 21 cm. *Paperback cover design.*

Henry, Joseph Bennet. *Fulfillment in Marriage.* Westwood, NJ: Fleming H. Revell, [1966]. 160 p., 21 cm. *Dust jacket design.*

Henry, Matthew. *Matthew Henry's Commentary on the Four Gospels.* Unabridged, with complete Bible text. New York: Fleming H. Revell, [n.d.]. 24 cm. *Dust jacket design.*

——. *Matthew Henry's Commentary on the Whole Bible . . . with Practical Remarks and Observations.* 6 vols. New York: Fleming H. Revell [n.d.]. 23 cm. *Dust jacket design.*

——. *The Secret of Communion with God.* Edited by Elisabeth Elliot. [Westwood, NJ]: Fleming H. Revell, [1963]. 120 p., 21 cm. *Dust jacket design.*

Herold, J. Christopher. *Bonaparte in Egypt.* New York: Harper & Row, [1962]. 424 p., 25 cm. *Dust jacket design.*

Hersey, John. *The Wall.* Giant Cardinal Edition, GC12. New York: Pocket Books, [1954]. 706 p., 16 cm. *Paperback cover design.*

Herzog, Jacob David. *A People That Dwells Alone: Speeches and Writings of Yaacov Herzog.* Edited by Misha Louvish. New York: Sanhedrin Press, 1975. 283 p., 22 cm. *Dust jacket design.*

High, Stanley. *Billy Graham: The Personal Story of the Man, His Message, and His Mission.* New York: McGraw-Hill, [1956]. 274 p., 22 cm. *Dust jacket design.*

Hofmann, Hans. *The Theology of Reinhold Niebuhr.* Translated by Louise Pettibone Smith. New York: Scribner, 1956. viii, 269 p., 22 cm. *Dust jacket design.*

Hopkins, Kenneth. *English Poetry: A Short History.* Philadelphia: Lippincott, [1963]. 568 p., 22 cm. *Dust jacket design.*

Hovey, E. Paul, comp. *The Treasury for Special Days and Occasions: Inspirational Anecdotes, Quotations, and Illustrations.* [Westwood, NJ]: Fleming H. Revell, [1961]. 317 p., 22 cm. *Dust jacket design.*

——. *The Treasury of Inspirational Anecdotes, Quotations, and Illustrations*. [Westwood, NJ]: Fleming H. Revell, [1959]. 316 p., 22 cm. *Dust jacket design.*

Howard, John Tasker. *The World's Great Operas*. New York: Modern Library, [1959]. 572 p., 19 cm. *Dust jacket design.*

Howe, Irving, and Eliezer Greenberg, eds. *A Treasury of Yiddish Stories*. With drawings by Ben Shahn. New York: Viking Press, 1954. 630 p., 22 cm. *Dust jacket design.*

Hume, Robert Ernest. *The World's Living Religions, with Special Reference to Their Sacred Scriptures and in Comparison with Christianity: An Historical Sketch*. Rev. ed. New York: Scribner, [1959]. 335 p., 20 cm. *Dust jacket design.*

Humphreys, Christmas, ed. *The Wisdom of Buddhism*. New York: Random House, [1961]. 280 p., 22 cm. *Dust jacket design.*

Hutchison, Bruce. *Canada: Tomorrow's Giant*. New York: Knopf, 1957. 325 p., 22 cm. *Dust jacket design*

Innes, Hammond. *Harvest of Journeys*. [1st American ed.] New York: Knopf, 1960. 305 p., 22 cm. *Dust jacket design.*

Irving, Washington. *Astoria: or, Anecdotes of an Enterprise Beyond the Rocky Mountains*. Introduction by William H. Goetzmann. Keystone Western Americana Series, KB 37–38. 2 vols. Philadelphia: Lippincott, 1961. 21 cm. *Dust jacket design; also issued as paperback edition.*

Jacob, Edmond. *Theology of the Old Testament*. Translated by Arthur W. Heathcote and Philip J. Allcock. New York: Harper & Row, 1958. 368 p., 22 cm. *Dust jacket design.*

James, Thomas. *Three Years Among the Indians and Mexicans*. The 1846 ed., unabridged. Introduction by A. P. Nasatir. Keystone Western Americana Series, KB 51. Philadelphia: Lippincott, [1962]. 173 p., 21 cm. *Dust jacket design; also issued as paperback edition.*

Jenkins, Elizabeth. *Elizabeth the Great*. 1st American ed. New York: Coward-McCann, [1959]. 336 p., 22 cm. *Dust jacket design.*

Johnson, Edna, et al. *Anthology of Children's Literature*. With black and white illustrations by Fritz Eichenberg and full color paintings by N.C. Wyeth. [3rd rev. ed.]. Boston: Houghton Mifflin, 1959. xxxv, 1,239 p., 25 cm. *Binding design.*

Juvenal. *The Satires of Juvenal*. Translated by Rolfe Humphries. Bloomington: Indiana University Press, 1958. 186 p., 20 cm. *Dust jacket design; also issued as paperback edition.*

Kampf, Avram. *Contemporary Synagogue Art: Developments in the United States, 1945–1965*. Philadelphia: Jewish Publication Society of America, 1966. vii, 276 p., 29 cm. *Dust jacket design; binding design.*

Kaplan, Mordecai Menahem. *The Purpose and Meaning of Jewish Existence: A People in the Image of God*. Philadelphia: Jewish Publication Society of America, 1964. x, 326 p., 22 cm. *Dust jacket design.*

Kates, Frederick Ward. *A Moment Between Two Eternities*. Harper ChapelBooks, CB 10. New York: Harper & Row, [1965]. xi, 189 p., 21 cm. *Paperback cover design.*

Kauffman, Donald T. *The Dictionary of Religious Terms*. Westwood, NJ: Fleming H. Revell, [1967]. 445 p., 24 cm. *Dust jacket design.*

——, comp. *The Treasury of Religious Verse*. [Westwood, NJ]: Fleming H. Revell, [1962]. 371 p., 22 cm. *Dust jacket design.*

Kennedy, Gerald Hamilton. *The Parables: Sermons on the Stories Jesus Told*. Harper ChapelBooks, CB 35.

New York: Harper & Row, 1967. vii, 213 p., 21 cm. *Paperback cover design.*

Kennedy, John Fitzgerald. *Profiles in Courage.* Memorial ed. New York: Harper & Row, [1964]. 287 p., 24 cm. *Lettering for band across dust jacket.*

Kepler, Thomas Samuel. *The Book of Revelation: A Commentary for Laymen.* New York: Oxford University Press, 1957. 232 p., 21 cm. *Dust jacket design.*

Kuchler-Silberman, Lena. *One Hundred Children.* Adapted from the Hebrew by David C. Gross. Garden City, NY: Doubleday, 1961. 288 p., 22 cm. *Dust jacket design.*

King, Clarence. *Mountaineering in the Sierra Nevada.* The 1872 ed., unabridged. Introduction by Thurman Wilkins. Keystone Western Americana Series, KB56. Philadelphia: Lippincott, 1963. 292 p., 21 cm. *Dust jacket design; also issued as paperback edition.*

Knobel, Peter S., ed. *Gates of the Seasons: A Guide to the Jewish Year.* Illustrated by Ismar David. New York: Central Conference of American Rabbis, 1983. ix, 208 p., 23 cm. *Paperback cover design; illustrations; chapter titles; end papers.*

Knuth, Donald Ervin. *3:16: Bible Texts Illuminated.* Madison, WI: A-R Editions, 1991. 268 p., 23 cm. *Illustration for Leviticus 3:16.*

Koenig, Oskar. *Pori Tupu.* Translated from the German by the author and Oliver Coburn. New York: McGraw-Hill, [1954]. 236 p., 21 cm. *Dust jacket design.*

Kokenes, Violeta Constantine. *On Wings of Faith.* New York: Random House, [1960]. 244 p., 21 cm. *Dust jacket design.*

Lanczkowski, Günter. *Sacred Writings: A Guide to the Literature of Religions.* Translated by Stanley Godman. Harper ChapelBooks, CB21H. New York: Harper & Row, [1966]. 147 p., 21 cm. *Paperback cover design.*

Lange, Jule. *The Seducer.* New York: Random House, [1960]. 407 p., 21 cm. *Dust jacket design*

La Sor, William Sanford. *Great Personalities of the New Testament: Their Lives and Times.* [Westwood, NJ]: Fleming H. Revell, [1961]. 192 p., 21 cm. *Dust jacket design.*

——. *Great Personalities of the Old Testament: Their Lives and Times.* [Westwood, NJ]: Fleming H. Revell, [1959]. 192 p., 21 cm. *Dust jacket design.*

Latourette, Kenneth Scott. *Christianity Through the Ages.* Harper ChapelBooks, CB1. New York: Harper & Row, [1965]. xiii, 321 p., 21 cm. *Paperback cover design.*

Laubach, Frank Charles. *War of Amazing Love.* Westwood, NJ: Fleming H. Revell, [1965]. 150 p., 21 cm. *Dust jacket design.*

Leach, Maria. *The Rainbow Book of American Folk Tales and Legends.* Illustrated by Marc Simont. Cleveland: World Publishing Co., [1958]. 318 p., 29 cm. *Lettering for title.*

Leeuw, Gerardus van der. *Religion in Essence and Manifestation.* Translated by J. E. Turner. 2 vols. Harper Torchbooks, TB100–101. New York: Harper & Row, [1963]. 21 cm. *Paperback cover design.*

Leithäuser, Joachim G. *Inventors' Progress.* Translated from the German by Michael Bullock. Cleveland: World Publishing Co., [1959]. 286 p., 25 cm. *Dust jacket design.*

Leonard, Jonathan N. *Exploring Science*. Illustrated by Louis Darling and I. N. Steinberg. Cleveland: World Publishing Co., [1959]. 318 p., 29 cm. *Lettering for dust jacket.*

Levy, Gertrude Rachel. *The Gate of Horn: A Study of the Religious Conceptions of the Stone Age and Their Influence Upon European Thought*. Harper Torchbooks, TB 10. New York: Harper & Row, 1963. xxxii, 349 p., 21 cm. *Paperback cover design.*

Lewis, Meriwether. *The Lewis and Clark Expedition*. Introduction by Archibald Hanna. 3 vols. Keystone Western American Series, KB 34–36. Philadelphia: Lippincott, [1961]. xxxi, 889 p., 21 cm. *Dust jacket design; also issued as paperback edition.*

Lewis, Robert. *Method – or Madness?* With an introduction by Harold Clurman. New York: French, [1958]. 165 p., 21 cm. *Dust jacket design.*

Liber Librorum. [Stockholm: Distributed by the Royal Library], 1955. 1 portfolio. 34 cm. *Page design specimen (4 p.) for Genesis 1:1–31, 2:1–12.*

Liles, Lester R., comp. *Streams of Healing: A Book of Comfort*. [Westwood, NJ]: Fleming H. Revell, [1958]. 60 p., 21 cm. *Dust jacket design.*

Lippmann, Walter. *The Communist World and Ours*. Boston: Little, Brown, [1959]. 56 p., 20 cm. *Dust jacket design.*

——. *Essays in the Public Philosophy*. Boston: Little, Brown, [1955]. 189 p., 22 cm. *Dust jacket design.*

Literature in the Making (series):
See entries for William Earl Buckler, John Gassner, and W. Walker Gibson.

London, Jack. *The Sun-Dog Trail, and Other Stories*. World Junior Library. Cleveland: World Publishing Co., [1951]. 224 p., 21 cm. *Dust jacket design.*

Longsworth, Polly. *I, Charlotte Forten, Black and Free*. New York: T. Y. Crowell, [1970]. 248 p., 21 cm. *Dust jacket lettering.*

Luther, Martin. *Martin Luther on the Bondage of the Will. A New Translation of De Servo Arbitrio (1525) Martin Luther's Reply to Erasmus of Rotterdam*, by J. I. Packer and O. R. Johnston. [Westwood, NJ]: Fleming H. Revell, [1957]. 322 p., 21 cm. *Dust jacket design.*

Machlis, Joseph. *American Composers of Our Time*. New York: T. Y. Crowell, [1963]. 237 p., 23 cm. *Dust jacket design.*

McGovern, James. *Fräulein*. New York: Crown Publishers, [1956]. 312 p., 22 cm. *Dust jacket design.*

MacGregor, Geddes. *Introduction to Religious Philosophy*. Boston: Houghton Mifflin, 1959. 366 p., 22 cm. *Paperback cover design.*

MacLeish, Archibald. *"J. B.": A Play in Verse*. Boston: Houghton Mifflin, 1957. 153 p., 23 cm. *Dust jacket design; title page and endpaper designs.*

McPherson, Nenien C. *The Power of a Purpose*. [Westwood, NJ]: Fleming H. Revell, [1959]. 156 p., 21 cm. *Dust jacket design.*

Maimonides, Moses, and Shlomo Pines, ed. and trans. *The Guide of the Perplexed*. [Chicago]: University of Chicago Press, 1963. 658 p., 26 cm. *Hebrew lettering for binding.*

Mandat-Grancey, Edmond, Baron de, ed. *Cow-boys and Colonels: Narrative of a Journey Across the Prairie and Over the Black Hills of Dakota*. Translated by William Conn from the 1887 London ed., unabridged. Keystone Western Americana Series, KB55. Philadelphia: Lippincott, 1963. 352 p., 21 cm. *Dust jacket design; also issued as paperback edition.*

Marblestone, Howard, and Harry M. Orlinsky. *The Legacy of Ancient Israel: A Syllabus*. New York: National Council of Jewish Women, 1975. iv, 26 p., 28 cm. *Paperback cover design.*

Marcy, Randolph Barnes. *Thirty Years of Army Life on the Border*. Introduction by Edward S. Wallace. Reprint of 1866 ed., unabridged. Keystone Western Americana Series, KB54. Philadelphia: Lippincott, 1963. xiv, 402 p., 21 cm. *Dust jacket design; also issued as paperback edition.*

Marriott, Alice Lee. *Indians on Horseback*. Drawings by Margaret Lefranc. New York: T. Y. Crowell, 1968. vii, 136 p., 21 cm. *Dust jacket design.*

Marryat, Frank. *Mountains and Molehills, or, Recollections of a Burnt Journal*. Reprint of the 1855 ed., unabridged. Introduction by Robin W. Winks. Keystone Western Americana Series, KB49. Philadelphia: Lippincott, [1962]. 233 p., 21 cm. *Dust jacket design; also issued as paperback edition.*

Marshall, Peter. *The Prayers of Peter Marshall*. Edited and with prefaces by Catherine Marshall. New York: McGraw-Hill, [1954]. 243 p., 21 cm. *Dust jacket design.*

Martin, Peter. *The Building*. Boston: Little, Brown, [1960]. 378 p., 22 cm. *Dust jacket design.*

Maslin, Simeon, ed. *Gates of Mitzvah: A Guide to the Jewish Life Cycle*. New York: Central Conference of American Rabbis, 1979. x, 166 p., 23 cm. *Illustration; lettering for dust jacket; chapter headings and title.*

Mathews, Basil Joseph. *Paul the Dauntless*. [Westwood, NJ]: Fleming H. Revell, [1959]. 375 p., 21 cm. *Dust jacket design.*

Maugham, W. Somerset. *Of Human Bondage*. Modern Library paperback, P16. New York: Random House, [1956]. 760 p., 19 cm. *Paperback cover design.*

Maynard, Theodore. *Great Catholics in American History*. Garden City, NY: Doubleday, 1957. 261 p., 22 cm. *Dust jacket design.*

Mead, Frank Spencer, ed. *Communion Messages*. [Westwood, NJ]: Fleming H. Revell, [1961]. 123 p., 21 cm. *Dust jacket design.*

———. *The March of Eleven Men*. [Westwood, NJ]: Fleming H. Revell, 1960. 236 p., 21 cm. *Dust jacket design.*

———. *Who's Who in the Bible: 250 Bible Biographies*. Harper ChapelBooks, CB25H. New York: Harper & Row, [1966]. 250 p., 20 cm. *Paperback cover design.*

Meek, Theophile James. *Hebrew Origins*. [Rev. ed.] Harper Torchbooks, TB69. New York: Harper & Row, [1960]. xv, 240 p., 21 cm. *Paperback cover design.*

Mehta, Ved. *The New Theologian*. New York: Harper & Row, [1966]. 217 p., 22 cm. *Dust jacket design.*

Meiss, Millard. *Painting in Florence and Siena after the Black Death: The Arts, Religion and Society in the Mid-Fourteenth Century*. Harper Torchbooks, TB1148. New York: Harper & Row, 1964. xii, 195 p., [42] leaves of plates, 21 cm. *Paperback cover design.*

Meltzer, Milton. *Tongue of Flame: The Life of Lydia Maria Child*. New York: T. Y. Crowell, [1965]. 210 p., 21 cm. *Dust jacket design.*

Mielke, Arthur W. *This is Protestantism*. [Westwood, NJ]: Fleming H. Revell, [1961]. 127 p., 24 cm. *Dust jacket design.*

Miers, Earl Schenck. *Mark Twain on the Mississippi*. Illustrated by Robert Frankenberg. Cleveland: World Publishing Co., [1957]. 246 p., 22 cm. *Lettering for dust jacket.*

——. *The Rainbow Book of American History*. Illustrated by James Daugherty. Cleveland, World Publishing Co., [1955]. 319 p., 29 cm. *Dust jacket design.*

Moore, Doris Langley-Levy. *The Late Lord Byron: Posthumous Dramas*. Philadelphia: Lippincott, [1961]. viii, 542 p., 24 cm. *Dust jacket design.*

Moravia, Alberto. *A Ghost at Noon*. Translated by Angus Davidson. New York: Farrar, Straus and Young, [1955]. 247 p., 22 cm. *Dust jacket design.*

Morgan, George Campbell. *The Analyzed Bible*. Westwood, NJ: Fleming H. Revell, [1964]. viii, 600 p., 22 cm. *Dust jacket design.*

——. *An Exposition of the Whole Bible: Chapter by Chapter in One Volume*. Westwood, NJ: Fleming H. Revell, 1959. 542 p., 21 cm. *Dust jacket design.*

——. *The Unfolding Message of the Bible: The Harmony and Unity of the Scriptures*. [Westwood, NJ]: Fleming H. Revell, [1961]. 416 p., 22 cm. *Dust jacket design.*

Morison, Samuel Eliot. *Freedom in Contemporary Society*. Boston: Little, Brown, [1956]. 156 p., 21 cm. *Dust jacket design.*

Morton, Frederic. *The Witching Ship*. New York: Random House, 1960. 271 p., 21 cm. *Dust jacket design.*

Moskin, Marietta D. *In the Name of God: Religion in Everyday Life*. New York: Atheneum, 1980. xiii, 185 p., 24 cm. *Dust jacket lettering.*

Muir, Robert. *The Sprig of Hemlock: A Novel About Shays' Rebellion*. New York: Longmans, Green, 1957. 314 p., 21 cm. *Dust jacket design.*

Munson, Gorham Bert. *Penobscot: Down East Paradise*. With woodcuts by Carroll Thayer Berry. Philadelphia: Lippincott, [1959]. 399 p., 22 cm. *Dust jacket design.*

Neusner, Jacob. *Defining Judaism: A Syllabus*. New York: National Council of Jewish Women, 1975. iv, 26 p., 28 cm. *Paperback cover design.*

Newman, Louis I., ed. *The Talmudic Anthology: Tales and Teachings of the Rabbis; A Collection of Parables, Folk-Tales, Fables, Aphorism, Epigrams, Sayings, Anecdotes, Proverbs and Exegetical Interpretations*, selected and edited by Louis I. Newman, in collaboration with Samuel Spitz. [New York]: Behrman House, [1962]. xxxiv, 570 p., 24 cm. *Dust jacket design.*

Nolen, Barbara. *Merry Hearts and Bold*. Illustrations by Fritz Kredel. Boston: D. C. Heath, 1955. 437 p., 23 cm. *Lettering for cover.*

Oates, Whitney Jennings, ed. *The Stoic and Epicurean Philosophers: The Complete Extant Writings of Epicurus, Epictetus, Lucretius and Marcus Aurelius*. New York: Random House, [1956]. xxvi, 627 p., 24 cm. *Dust jacket design.*

O'Hara, John. *A Family Party*. New York: Random House, [1956]. 64 p., 21 cm. *Dust jacket design.*

Outler, Albert Cook. *Psychotherapy and the Christian Message*. Harper ChapelBooks, CB26K. New York: Harper & Row, 1966. 286 p., 21 cm. *Cover design.*

Ovid. *The Loves; The Art of Beauty; The Remedies for Love; and The Art of Love*. Translated by Rolfe Humphries. A Midland book, MB2. Bloomington: Indiana University Press, 1957. 206 p., 20 cm. *Dust jacket design; also issued as paperback edition.*

——. *Metamorphoses*. Translated by Rolfe Humphries. Bloomington: Indiana University Press, 1955. 401 p., 20 cm. *Dust jacket design; also issued as paperback edition.*

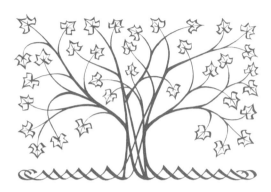

Ozment, Robert Varnell. *But God Can*. [Westwood, NJ]: Fleming H. Revell, [1962]. 126 p., 21 cm. *Dust jacket design.*

——. *Happy is the Man*. [Westwood, NJ]: Fleming H. Revell, [1963]. 128 p., 21 cm. *Dust jacket design.*

——. *There's Always Hope*. Westwood, NJ: Fleming H. Revell, [1964]. 64 p., 20 cm. *Dust jacket design.*

Packe, Michael St. John. *Orsini: The Story of a Conspirator*. 1st American ed. Boston: Little, Brown, [1958]. 313 p., 22 cm. *Dust jacket design.*

Parker, Elinor Milnor, comp. *100 Poems About People*. Illustrated by Ismar David. New York: T.Y. Crowell, [1955]. 234 p., 21 cm. *Dust jacket design; illustrations; chapter titles.*

Parmelee, Alice. *A Guidebook to the Bible*. Harper ChapelBooks, CB15L. New York: Harper & Row, [1965]. xi, 331 p., 21 cm. *Paperback cover design.*

Pascal, Blaise. *Les Pensées*. Translated by Martin Turnell. Illustrated by Ismar David. Typography by Charles E. Scaggs. Bloomfield, CT: Printed for the members of the Limited Editions Club, 1971. xix, 184 p., 30 cm. *Binding design; illustrations; lettering; decorative elements.*

Patai, Irene. *The Valley of God*. New York: Random House, [1956]. 351 p., 21 cm. *Dust jacket design.*

Pattie, James O. *The Personal Narrative of James O. Pattie*. Reprint of the 1831 ed., unabridged. Introduction by William H. Goetzmann. Keystone Western Americana Series, KB50. Philadelphia: Lippincott, [1962]. 269 p., 21 cm. *Dust jacket design; also issued as paperback edition.*

Payne, Robert. *The Splendor of France*. New York: Harper & Row, [1963]. x, 207 p., 25 cm. *Dust jacket design.*

Payne, Robert. *The Splendor of Israel*. New York: Harper & Row, [1963]. xii, 222 p., 25 cm. *Dust jacket design.*

Peare, Catherine Owens. *The Herbert Hoover Story*. New York: T.Y. Crowell, [1965]. 247 p., 21 cm. *Dust jacket design.*

Peattie, Donald Culross. *The Rainbow Book of Nature*. Illustrated by Rudolf Freund. Cleveland: World Publishing Co., 1957. 319 p., 29 cm. *Lettering for dust jacket.*

Pegis, Jessie Corrigan. *A Practical Catholic Dictionary*. Garden City, NY: Hanover House, [1957]. 258 p., 22 cm. *Dust jacket design.*

Pelikan, Jaroslav Jan. *Obedient Rebels: Catholic Substance and Protestant Principle in Luther's Reformation*. New York: Harper & Row, 1964. 212 p., 24 cm. *Dust jacket design.*

Petuchowski, Jakob Josef. *Prayerbook Reform in Europe; the Liturgy of European Liberal and Reform Judaism*. Foreword by Solomon B. Freehof. New York: World Union for Progressive Judaism, [1968]. xxii, 407 p., 25 cm. *Dust jacket and cover design.*

Pfeiffer, Robert Henry. *The Books of the Old Testament*. Harper ChapelBooks, CB11. New York: Harper & Row, [1965]. 335 p., 21 cm. *Paperback cover design.*

Phelan, Mary Kay. *The Fourth of July*. Illustrated by Symeon Shimon. New York: T. Y. Crowell, [1966]. 1 vol. (unpaged), 22 cm. *Design and lettering of dust jacket; design of title and half-title pages.*

Pittenger, William Norman. *Loving Says it All*. New York: Pilgrim Press, 1978. 126 p., 22 cm. *Dust jacket design.*

Pitts, John. *Faith Healing: Fact or Fiction?* [Westwood, NJ]: Fleming H. Revell, [1961]. 159 p., 22 cm. *Dust jacket design.*

Plaut, W. Gunther. *The Growth of Reform Judaism: American and European Sources until 1948*. Foreword by Rabbi Jacob K. Shankman. New York: World Union for Progressive Judaism, [1965]. 383 p., 25 cm. *Dust jacket; binding design.*

——. *The Rise of Reform Judaism: A Sourcebook of its European Origins*. Preface by Solomon B. Freehof. New York: World Union for Progressive Judaism, [1963]. xxii, 288 p., 25 cm. *Dust jacket design; binding design.*

Plotz, Helen. comp. *The Earth is the Lord's: Poems of the Spirit*. Illustrated with wood engravings by Clare Leighton. New York: Crowell, [1965]. xiv, 223 p., 23 cm. *Dust jacket design.*

——, comp. *Poems from the German*. Drawings by Ismar David. Poems of the World series. New York: T. Y. Crowell, [1967]. vii, 181 p., 21 cm. *Book design; dust jacket design; illustrations; decorative elements.*

Pool, David de Sola, ed. *The Traditional Prayer Book*. New Hyde Park, NY: University Books by arrangement with Behrman House, 1960. xvi, 879 p., 27 cm. *Dust jacket, box and binding design; title page lettering; ornamental initials; also issued in smaller (22 cm) format.*

Popper, Karl Raimund, Sir. *The Logic of Scientific Discovery*. Harper Torchbooks, TB576. New York: Harper & Row, 1965. 479 p., 21 cm. *Paperback cover design.*

——. *The Poverty of Historicism*. Harper Torchbooks, TB1126. New York: Harper & Row, 1964. x, 166 p., 21 cm. *Paperback cover design.*

Potts, George C. *Background to the Bible: An Introduction*. Harper ChapelBooks, CB22G. New York: Harper & Row, [1966]. 162 p., 21 cm. *Paperback cover design.*

Pratt, Dorothy, and Richard Pratt. *A Guide to Early American Homes*. 2 vols. New York: McGraw-Hill, [1956]. 26 cm. *Dust jacket design.*

Price, Eugenia. *Early I Will Seek Thee, Journal of a Heart that Longed and Found*. [Westwood, NJ]: Fleming H. Revell, [1956]. 185 p., 22 cm. *Dust jacket design.*

Prize Articles 1954: The Benjamin Franklin Magazine Awards, administered by the University of Illinois. New York: Ballantine Books, 1954. 142 p., 21 cm. *Dust jacket design.*

Prosser, William Harrison. *Enemies and Friends*. Boston: Little, Brown, [1958]. 247 p., 21 cm. *Dust jacket design.*

Pynchon, Thomas. *V: A Novel*. Philadelphia: Lippincott, [1963]. 492 p., 22 cm. *Dust jacket design.*

Raymond, Jack. *Power at the Pentagon*. New York: Harper & Row, [1964]. xiv, 363 p., 25 cm. *Dust jacket design.*

Redding, David A. *The Miracles of Christ*. Westwood, NJ: Fleming H. Revell, [1964]. xiv, 186 p., 21 cm. *Dust jacket design.*

——. *The Parables He Told*. [Westwood, NJ]: Fleming H. Revell, [1962]. 177 p., 21 cm. *Dust jacket design.*

——. *Psalms of David*. [Westwood, NJ]: Fleming H. Revell, [1963]. xvii, 174 p., 21 cm. *Dust jacket design.*

Redpath, Alan. *The Making of a Man of God; Studies in the Life of David*. [Westwood, NJ]: Fleming H. Revell, [1962]. 256 p., 21 cm. *Dust jacket design.*

Reinfeld, Fred. *The Biggest Job in the World: The American Presidency*. New York: T. Y. Crowell, [1964]. 229 p., 21 cm. *Dust jacket design.*

——. *Chess: Win in Twenty Moves or Less*. New York: T. Y. Crowell, [1962]. 150 p., 21 cm. *Dust jacket design.*

——. *The Great Dissenters: Guardians of Their Country's Laws and Liberties*. New York: T. Y. Crowell, [1959]. 180 p., 21 cm. *Dust jacket design.*

Religious Paintings by the Great Masters. Introductory essay, "Christianity and Art," by Marvin Halverson. New York: Harry N. Abrams, [1954?] 1 portfolio ([8] p., [12] leaves of plates), 39 cm. *Cover design; decorative frames and initials.*

Ringelblum, Emanuel. *Notes from the Warsaw Ghetto: The Journal of Emmanuel Ringelblum*. Edited and translated by Jacob Sloan. New York: McGraw-Hill, [1958]. 369 p., 22 cm. *Dust jacket design*

Riverside Editions (series). Boston: Houghton Mifflin, [v.d.]. *Paperback cover designs and colophon design for series.*

Riverside Studies in Literature (series). Boston: Houghton Mifflin, [v.d.]. *Paperback cover designs for series.*

Robertson, Constance Noyes. *Go and Catch a Falling Star*. New York: Random House, [1957]. 368 p., 21 cm. *Dust jacket design.*

Robertson, Robert Blackwood. *Of Sheep and Men*. New York: Knopf, 1957. 308 p., 22 cm. *Dust jacket design.*

——. *Of Whales and Men*. New York: Knopf, 1954. 299 p., 22 cm. *Dust jacket design.*

Robins, Dorothy B. *Experiment in Democracy: The Story of U.S. Citizen Organizations in Forging the Charter of the United Nations*. New York: Parkside Press, [1971]. xx, 316 p., 24 cm. *Dust jacket design*

Rollins, Charlemae Hill. *They Showed the Way: Forty American Negro Leaders*. New York: T. Y. Crowell, [1964]. 165 p., 21 cm. *Dust jacket design.*

Rosowsky, Solomon. *The Cantillation of the Bible: The Five Books of Moses*. New York: Reconstructionist Press, 1957. 669 p., 26 cm. *Design of dust jacket, binding, title and half-titles.*

Roth, Cecil. *A History of the Marranos*. 2nd rev. ed. Jewish Publication Society Series, JP12. New York, Philadelphia: Meridian Books; Jewish Publication Society of America, [1959]. 424 p., 21 cm. *Dust jacket design.*

——. *The Jews in the Renaissance*. Philadelphia: Jewish Publication Society of America, 1959. 380 p., 22 cm. *Dust jacket design.*

——. *The Jews in the Renaissance*. 1st Harper Torchbook ed. Harper Torchbooks, TB834N. New York: Harper & Row, [1965]. xii, 378, 10 p., [8] leaves of plates, 21 cm. *Paperback cover design.*

Royal, Claudia. *Teaching Your Child about God*. [Westwood, NJ]: Fleming H. Revell, [1960]. 186 p., 21 cm. *Dust jacket design.*

Sacred Paintings by the Great Masters. Introductory essay, "Spiritual Values in Art," by Lee H. B. Malone. New York: Harry N. Abrams, [195-?]. 1 portfolio ([8] p., [12] leaves of plates), 39 cm. *Cover design; decorative frames and initials.*

Salinger, J. D. *The Catcher in the Rye*. 1st Modern Library ed. New York: Random House, 1958. 277 p., 19 cm. *Dust jacket design.*

Samuels, Gertrude. *B-G, Fighter of Goliaths: The Story of David Ben-Gurion*. New York: T.Y. Crowell, [1961]. 275 p., 21 cm. *Dust jacket design.*

Sandburg, Helga. *The Wheel of Earth*. [New York]: McDowell, Obolensky, [1958]. 396 p., 22 cm. *Dust jacket design.*

Sandlin, John Lewis. *Moments with the Master*. Westwood, NJ: Fleming H. Revell, 1961. 128 p., 17 cm. *Dust jacket design.*

——. *A Prayer for Every Day*. Westwood, NJ: Fleming H. Revell, 1958. 128 p., 17 cm. *Dust jacket design.*

Sarett, Lew R., et al. *Basic Principles of Speech*. 3rd ed. Boston: Houghton Mifflin, [1958]. 601 p., 25 cm. *Binding and endpaper designs.*

Savory, Teo. *The Landscape of Dreams: A Novel*. New York: G. Braziller, 1960. 311 p., 22 cm. *Dust jacket design.*

——. *The Single Secret: A Novel*. New York: G. Braziller, 1961. 318 p., 21 cm. *Dust jacket design.*

Schauss, Hayyim. *The Lifetime of a Jew Throughout the Ages of Jewish History*. Commission on Jewish Education of the Union of American Hebrew Congregations and the Central Conference of American Rabbis, Union Graded Series. New York: Union of American Hebrew Congregations, 1970. xiii, 332 p., 24 cm. *Paperback cover design.*

Scherer, Paul. *For We Have This Treasure*. 1st Harper ChapelBook ed., CB4. New York: Harper & Row, 1965. xii, 212 p., 21 cm. *Paperback cover design.*

Schiøtz, Aksel. *The Singer and His Art*. New York: Harper & Row, [1969]. xvi, 214 p., 22 cm. *Dust jacket design.*

Schleiermacher, Friedrich. *The Christian Faith*. Edited by H. R. Mackintosh and J. S. Stewart. 2 vols. Harper Torchbooks, TB108. New York: Harper & Row, 1963. 20 cm. *Paperback cover design.*

Schwartz, Harry, ed. *Russia Enters the 1960s: A Documentary Report on the 22nd Congress of the Communist Party of the Soviet Union*. Philadelphia: Lippincott, 1962. ix, 278 p., 22 cm. *Dust jacket design.*

Schwarz, Leo Walder, ed. *Great Ages and Ideas of the Jewish People*, by Salo W. Baron, et al. New York: Random House, [1956]. xxvii, 515 p., 22 cm. *Dust jacket design.*

Sedych, Andrei. *This Land of Israel*. Translated by Elizabeth Reynolds Hapgood. New York: Macmillan, [1967]. 244 p., 22 cm. *Dust jacket design.*

Shaw, Richard, comp., and ed. *The Bird Book*. New York: Frederick Warne, [1974]. 48 p., 24 cm. *Single illustration.*

——, comp., and ed. *The Cat Book*. New York: Frederick Warne, [1973]. 48 p., 24 cm. *Single illustration.*

——, comp., and ed. *The Fox Book*. New York: Frederick Warne, [1971]. 47 p., 24 cm. *Single illustration.*

——, comp., and ed. *The Frog Book*. New York: Frederick Warne, [1972]. 46 p., 24 cm. *Single illustration.*

——, comp., and ed. *The Owl Book*. New York: Frederick Warne, [1970]. 48 p., 24 cm. *Single illustration.*

Shulevitz, Uri. *The Secret Room*. New York: Farrar, Straus and Giroux, 1993. 1 vol. (unpaged), 27 cm. *Dust jacket lettering.*

Shumsky, Abraham, and Adaia Shumsky. *Olam Gadol*. Illustrated by Leo Glueckselig. 2 vols. New York: Union of American Hebrew Congregations, [1972–]. 22 cm. *Design of double page spread and Hebrew lettering for the "Peanuts" edition.*

Shuptrine, Hubert, and James Dickey. *Jericho: The South Beheld*. Birmingham, AL: Oxmoor House, 1974. 165 p., 33 cm. *Lettering for book cover and spine, half-titles and headings; dust jacket design.*

Simpson, Dorothy. *The Maine Islands in Story and Legend, from Material Compiled by the Maine Writers Research Club*. Philadelphia: Lippincott, [1960]. 256 p., 22 cm. *Dust jacket design.*

Smith, Bradford, and Marion Collins Smith. *Why We Behave Like Americans*. Philadelphia: Lippincott, [1957]. 322 p., 22 cm. *Dust jacket design.*

Solzhenitsyn, Aleksandr Isaevich. *The First Circle*. Translated from the Russian by Thomas P. Whitney. New York: Harper & Row, [1968]. xiii, 580 p., 25 cm. *Dust jacket design.*

Songs and Hymns: A Musical Supplement to Gates of Prayer. New York: American Conference of Cantors and Central Conference of American Rabbis, 1977. 24 p., 25 cm. *Hebrew titling; illustrations from* The Psalms *(1973).*

Speakman, Frederick Bruce. *Love is Something You Do*. [Westwood, NJ]: Fleming H. Revell, [1959]. 154 p., 22 cm. *Dust jacket design.*

Stafford, Jean. *The Mountain Lion*. New York: Popular Library, 1962. 174 p., 18 cm. *Dust jacket design.*

Stearns, Peter N. *Priest and Revolutionary: Lamennais and the Dilemma of French Catholicism*. New York: Harper & Row, [1967]. x, 209 p., 22 cm. *Dust jacket design.*

Stern, Chaim, ed. *Gates of Prayer: The New Union Prayerbook*. New York: Central Conference of American Rabbis, 1975. 779 pages in loose leaf binder, 29 cm. *Hebrew titling. Also issued in other formats with same lettering.*

Stevenson, Adlai E. *Putting First Things First: A Democratic View*. New York: Random House, 1960. 115 p., 21 cm. *Dust jacket design.*

Summerhayes, Martha. *Vanished Arizona*. Reprint of the 1908 ed., unabridged. Keystone Western Americana Series, KB57. Philadelphia: Lippincott, 1963. 257 p., 21 cm. *Dust jacket design; also issued as paperback edition.*

Swarthout, Glendon Fred. *They Came to Cordura*. New York: Random House, [1958]. 213 p., 21 cm. *Dust jacket design.*

Sweeney, John. *Skin Diving and Exploring Underwater*. New York: McGraw-Hill, [1955]. 176 p., 21 cm. *Dust jacket design.*

Taft, Philip. *Organized Labor in American History*. New York: Harper & Row, [1964]. xxi, 818 p., 24 cm. *Dust jacket design.*

Taves, Isabella. *The Quick Rich Fox*. New York: Random House, [1959]. 304 p., 21 cm. *Dust jacket design.*

Teller, Judd L. *Scapegoat of Revolution*. New York: Scribner, 1954. 352 p., 22 cm. *Dust jacket design.*

Tharp, Louise Hall. *Adventurous Alliance: The Story of the Agassiz Family of Boston*. Boston: Little, Brown, [1959]. 354 p., 22 cm. *Dust jacket design.*

Thomas, George Finger. *Religious Philosophies of the West*. New York: Scribner, [1965]. xviii, 454 p., 24 cm. *Dust jacket design.*

Thompson, Morton. *The Cry and the Covenant*. [Garden City, NY]: Doubleday, 1954. 469 p., 22 cm. *Dust jacket design.*

Thomsen, Alexander. *In the Name of Humanity*. Translated and adapted from the Danish by Maurice Michel. New York: Dutton, 1963. 229 p., 22 cm. *Dust jacket design.*

Thorbecke, Ellen Kolban. *Promised Land*. With photographs by Ellen Thorbecke. New York: Harper & Brothers, [1947]. 172 p., 24 cm. *Dust jacket design; cover design; illustrations; lettering.*

Tillich, Paul. *Systematic Theology*. 3 vols. in 1. [Chicago]: University of Chicago Press, [1967]. 442 p., 24 cm. *Dust jacket design.*

Tolstoy, Leo. *Great Short Works of Leo Tolstoy*. Translated by Louise and Aylmer Maude. Harper Perennial Classic, P 3071. New York: Harper & Row, [1967]. xviii, 685 p., 18 cm. *Paperback cover lettering.*

Tournier, Paul. *The Healing of Persons*. Translated by Edwin Hudson. New York: Harper & Row, [1965]. xx, 300 p., 22 cm. *Dust jacket design.*

——. *The Person Reborn*. Translated by Edwin Hudson. New York: Harper & Row, [1966]. vi, 248 p., 22 cm. *Dust jacket design.*

Trobisch, Walter, comp. *I Loved a Girl; Young Africans Speak: A Private Correspondence Between Two Young Africans and Their Pastor*. Harper ChapelBooks, CB12. New York: Harper & Row, [1965]. x, 109 p., 21 cm. *Paperback cover design.*

——. *I Married You*. New York: Harper & Row, [1971]. 135 p., 22 cm. *Dust jacket design.*

Trueblood, Elton. *The Common Ventures of Life: Marriage, Birth, Work, Death*. Harper ChapelBooks, CB3. New York: Harper, 1965. 124 p., 21 cm. *Paperback cover design.*

——. *The Predicament of Modern Man*. Harper ChapelBooks, CB37. New York: Harper & Row, 1967. x, 105 p., 21 cm. *Paperback cover design.*

Truman, Margaret, with Margaret Cousins. *Souvenir: Margaret Truman's Own Story*. New York: McGraw-Hill, [1956]. 365 p., 22 cm. *Dust jacket design.*

Twain, Mark. *Great Short Works of Mark Twain*. Edited, with an introduction, by Justin Kaplan. New York: Harper & Row, [1967]. xiv, 370 p., 18 cm. *Paperback cover lettering.*

The Typophiles. *Chapbook Commentary 26*. New York: The Typophiles, [1955]. 16 p., 18 cm. *Cover lettering and illustration on p. 2.*

Van Paassen, Pierre. *To Number Our Days*. New York: Scribner, [1964]. 404 p., 24 cm. *Dust jacket design.*

Vilnay, Zev. *The Guide to Israel*. Cleveland: World Publishing Co., 1960. 576 p., 17 cm. *Dust jacket design*.

Virgil. *The Aeneid; an Epic Poem of Rome*. Translated by L.R. Lind. Midland book, MB 45. Bloomington: Indiana University Press, 1963. xxiv, 301 p., 21 cm. *Paperback cover design*.

Vorspan, Albert. *Giants of Justice*. Illustrations by Ismar David. New York: Union of American Hebrew Congregations, 1960. 260 p., 21 cm. *Dust jacket and binding design; illustrations*.

Walker, Harold Blake. *Power to Manage Yourself*. Harper ChapelBooks, CB 39. New York: Harper & Row, [1967]. x, 237 p., 21 cm. *Paperback cover design*.

Wallace, Helen Kingsbury. *Meditations on New Testament Symbols: Devotions for Women*. [Westwood, NJ]: Fleming H. Revell, [1962]. 127 p., 21 cm. *Dust jacket design*.

Walsh, William Thomas. *Our Lady of Fátima*. Introduction by William C. McGrath. Doubleday Image Book, D 1. Garden City, NY: Image Books, [1954]. 223 p., 18 cm. *Lettering for paperback cover*.

Weidman, Jerome. *Before You Go*. New York: Random House, [1960]. 437 p., 22 cm. *Dust jacket design*.

Weltner, Charles Longstreet. *Southerner*. Philadelphia: Lippincott, 1966. 188 p., 22 cm. *Dust jacket design*.

Wertenbaker, Lael Tucker. *Death of a Man*. New York: Random House, 1957. 180 p., 21 cm. *Dust jacket design*.

West, Anthony. *Heritage*. New York: Random House, [1955]. 309 p., 21 cm. *Dust jacket design*.

——. *The Trend is Up*. New York: Random House, [1960]. 474 p., 21 cm. *Dust jacket design*.

Williams, Daniel Day. *God's Grace and Man's Hope: An Interpretation of the Christian Life in History*. Harper ChapelBooks, CB 17J. New York: Harper & Row, [1965]. 215 p., 21 cm. *Paperback cover design*.

Wilson, Dorothy Clarke. *The Gifts: A Story of the Boyhood of Jesus*. New York: McGraw-Hill, [1957]. 282 p., 21 cm. *Dust jacket design*.

Wirt, Mildred. *Ghost Gables*. World Junior Library. Cleveland: World Publishing Co., [n.d.]. 205 p., 21 cm. *Dust jacket design*.

Wirt, Sherwood Eliot. *The Social Conscience of the Evangelical*. New York: Harper & Row, [1968]. xiii, 177 p., 22 cm. *Dust jacket design*.

Wise, Carroll A. *Mental Health and the Bible: How to Relate the Insights of the Bible to the Recent Findings of Psychology and Medicine*. Harper ChapelBooks, CB 23H. [New York]: Harper & Row, [1966]. 168 p., 21 cm. *Paperback cover design*.

Wiseman, Adele. *The Sacrifice: A Novel*. New York: Viking Press, 1956. 346 p., 23 cm. *Dust jacket design*.

Wolfe, Thomas. *The Letters of Thomas Wolfe*. Collected and edited, with an introduction and explanatory text, by Elizabeth Nowell. New York: Scribner, 1956. xviii, 797 p., 25 cm. *Dust jacket design*.

Wordsworth, William. *Poems of William Wordsworth*, selected by Elinor Parker, with wood engravings by Diana Bloomfield. New York: T.Y. Crowell, 1964. 147 p., 21 cm. *Dust jacket design*.

Wylie, Ida Alexa Ross. *Claire Serrat: A Novel*. New York: Putnam, [1959]. 252 p., 21 cm. *Dust jacket design*.

Yacine, Kateb. *Nedjma: A Novel*. Translated from the French by Richard Howard. New York: G. Braziller, 1961. 344 p., 21 cm. *Dust jacket design*.

Yehuda, Zvi A. *Job: Ordeal, Defiance and Healing: A Study Guide.* Hadassah Study Series. New York: Hadassah, the Women's Zionist Organization of America, 1990. vii, 119 p., 23 cm. *Paperback cover design.*

Yep, Laurence. *The Butterfly Boy.* Pictures by Jeanne M. Lee. New York: Farrar, Straus and Giroux, 1993. 1 vol. (unpaged), 29 cm. *Dust jacket lettering.*

Young, Edward J. *The Study of Old Testament Theology Today.* [Westwood, NJ]: Fleming H. Revell, [1959]. 112 p., 20 cm. *Dust jacket design.*

Youngdahl, Reuben K. *Turbulent World, Tranquil God.* Westwood, NJ: Fleming H. Revell, [1958]. 157 p., 22 cm. *Dust jacket design.*

Zimmerman, John Edward. *Dictionary of Classical Mythology.* New York: Harper & Row, [1964]. xx, 300 p., 21 cm. *Dust jacket design.*

Zimmern, Alfred Eckhard, Sir. *The Greek Commonwealth; Politics and Economics in Fifth-Century Athens.* New York: Modern Library, [1956]. xi, 487 p., 19 cm. *Dust jacket design.*

Fifteen hundred copies
of this book have been printed on Mohawk Superfine
paper at The Studley Press.

ABCDEFGHIJKLMNOPQRSTUVWXYZ
12345 abcdefghijklmnopqrstuvwxyz 67890

The text type is
Galliard, designed by Matthew Carter,
with display typeset in

ABCDEFGHIJKLMNOPQRSTUVWXYZ
12345 abcdefghijklmnopqrstuvwxyz 67890

David Classic, David Humanistic,
and Inscripta, all designed by
Ismar David,

ABCDEFGHIJKLMNOPQRSTUVWXYZ
12345 abcdefghijklmnopqrstuvwxyz 67890

specially digitized for this book
by Helen Brandshaft.
Editorial assistance by Sandra Markham.

ABCDEFGHIJKLMNOPQRSTUVWXYZ
12345 abcdefghijklmnopqrstuvwxyz 67890

Book design by Jerry Kelly.